THE HORSE

FROM ARABIA TO ROYAL ASCOT

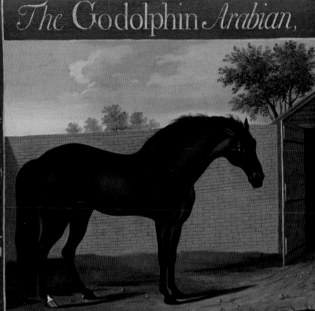

THE HORSE

FROM ARABIA TO ROYAL ASCOT

John Curtis and Nigel Tallis
With the assistance of Astrid Johansen

THE BRITISH MUSEUM PRESS

This book is published to accompany the exhibition at the British Museum from 24 May to 30 September 2012.

This exhibition has been made possible by the provision of insurance through the Government Indemnity Scheme. The British Museum would like to thank the Department for Culture, Media and Sport, and Arts Council England for providing and arranging this indemnity.

First published in 2012 by The British Museum Press
A division of The British Museum Company Ltd
38 Russell Square, London WC1B 3QQ
britishmuseum.org/publishing

A catalogue record for this book is available from the British Library

ISBN 978 0 7141 1183 4 (pbk)
ISBN 978 0 7141 1185 8 (cased)
ISBN 978 0 7141 1186 5 (slip cased)

Designed by Price Watkins
Printed in Italy by Graphicom srl

Most of the objects illustrated in this book are from the collection of the British Museum (BM). The registration numbers for these objects can be found in the corresponding caption. Further information about the Museum and its collection can be found at britishmuseum.org.

Half-title page: The Godolphin Arabian, Thomas Butler, *c.* 1750–5. See cat. 208.
Frontispiece: Three galloping horses (detail), *c.* 1550. See cat. 152.
Title page: Stamp seal with a winged horse, 4th century. See cat. 126.
Above right: Detail from a ewer with inlaid decoration, *c.* 1232. See cat. 135.
Opposite: Rein-ring decorated with a figure of an ass, *c.* 2600 BC. See cat. 2.
P. 8: Mid-eighteenth century portrait on paper of the grandson of Abul Hasan Qutb Shah (1672–1687), shown riding a richly equipped stallion and carrying a hawk. His grandfather, the last ruler of the Qutb Shahi dynasty of Golconda in India was defeated by the Mughal emperor Aurangzeb in 1687. BM 1974,0617,0.9.

Contents

Foreword

IT IS WELL KNOWN that the horse has played a crucial role in the development of civilization, and that a close bond exists between horses and men. This was recognized by the Prophet Muhammad, may peace be upon him, but respect and admiration for horses is not confined to the Muslim region. People all over the world and belonging to many different faiths revere the horse, and it is because of this widespread and deeply rooted interest that it is so important to organize informative exhibitions on the subject. In the long history of the horse Saudi Arabia has played an important role, and the region had given its name to what is now known as 'the Arabian horse'. Important discoveries have recently been made in Saudi Arabia which might shed light on the early history of this horse, and the many rock drawings of horses throughout the kingdom are of absorbing interest. I am proud of the fact that King Abdulaziz al-Saud is sometimes known as 'the last horseman' on account of the fact that he was the last leader in history to unite a country on horseback.

Horses have always been an important part of Arabian culture, and I personally have had a lifelong interest in and association with horses. For many years I harboured an ambition to sponsor some definitive work on horses and horsemanship, and that ambition was realized through two splendid volumes entitled *Furusiyya* published by the King Abdulaziz Public Library in 1996. These volumes, edited by David Alexander, contained a series of authoritative essays about the history of the horse and a list of objects in museums around the world relating to the history of horses. Some of the objects in that catalogue are included in the present exhibition. Following on from the *Furusiyya* volumes it is gratifying that it was possible to organize a major international exhibition on the subject at the International Museum of the Horse in Kentucky Horse Park, from May to October 2010. The exhibition, entitled *A Gift from the Desert: the Art, History and Culture of the Arabian Horse* was accompanied by a beautiful catalogue by Sandra Olsen and Cynthia Culbertson. This comprehensive exhibition proved to be very popular, and made a great contribution to our knowledge not only about the history of the Arabian horse but about the history of horses in general. However, the exhibition did not travel and people in Europe did not have an opportunity to see it. I am therefore very pleased indeed that it has now been possible to arrange an exhibition on a similar subject in London. Of course it does not replicate the exhibition in Kentucky, nor does it cover quite the same ground, but this is a good thing as it gives us an opportunity to look at different aspects of the history of the Arabian horse and the context from which it emerged.

FAISSAL IBN ABDULLAH IBN MUHAMMAD AL-SAUD
Minister of Education
(Chairman of the Board of Trustees of the Saudi Equestrian Fund)

Supported by

الفروسية السعودية
SAUDI EQUESTRIAN

مؤسسة ليان للثقافة
Layan Cultural Foundation

JUDDMONTE

In association with the Saudi Commission for Tourism & Antiquities, the King Abdulaziz Arabian Horse Centre and the King Abdulaziz Public Library.

Foreword

THE COLLECTIONS of the British Museum are renowned around the world for their breadth and depth, which gives visitors an almost unrivalled opportunity to view objects not just in the context of the cultures which produced them but also in the context of other, related societies. Although on the whole the permanent exhibitions are not arranged by theme, many significant subjects and topics which have been of wide significance are well represented across the different departments of the museum. Horses are a case in point, and such is the wealth of the collection that they provide an ideal subject for a special exhibition. Our only concern, in view of the embarrassment of riches at our disposal, has been how to limit the exhibition so that it had a meaningful narrative and could tell in a comprehensible way one part of the very rich history of the horse. Conversations with HH Prince Faissal Ibn Abdullah Ibn Muhammad Al-Saud led us to focus on the story of the Arabian horse, which combines a significant Middle Eastern history with one of the most popular British pursuits.

The result is an exhibition that reviews the history of the horse in the Middle East in the ancient and Islamic periods in order to show the context from which the Arabian horse emerges. We then go on to look at the horse in the Arabian Peninsula itself, and describe how from the seventeeth century onwards many oriental stallions including Arabians were imported into Britain and bred with British and Irish mares to improve the speed and resilience of the native stock. The eventual result of this process was the Thoroughbred horse, and as is well known all modern Thoroughbred horses trace their ancestry back to just three stallions, the Godolphin Arabian, the Darley Arabian and the Byerley Turk. Amongst those involved in the introduction and breeding of oriental horses in Britain were Lady Anne Blunt and Wilfrid Scawen Blunt, and their story is included in the exhibition.

Nowadays in Britain, flat-racing and steeple-chasing are mostly restricted to Thoroughbreds, as opposed to equestrian events, where the competing horses are often Thoroughbreds crossed with other breeds. In addition, purebred Arabian horses are involved in events all around the world. In essence, then, the exhibition describes the history of the horse from its domestication in about 3500 BC down to modern flat-racing and equestrian events which are an important component of the Olympic Games. It is a happy coincidence that this exhibition is taking place in 2012 when the Olympic Games are being held in London.

Many of the objects in this exhibition come from the British Museum's own collection but these have been supplemented by loans from various institutions in Saudi Arabia, the United Kingdom and Switzerland, as well as several private individuals. We are most grateful to all of them for their generosity. We are also indebted to the organizers of the exhibition on the Arabian horse, *A Gift from the Desert,* held in the International Museum of the Horse in Kentucky Horse Park in the summer of 2010. It covered some of the same ground as this exhibition but the overall treatment of the subject is inevitably different. I would also like to pay tribute to the *Furusiyya* catalogue (1996), edited by David Alexander, which gathered a great deal of information about the history of horses and has been a source of inspiration ever since. Finally, we are most grateful to Prince Faissal, HRH Prince Khalid bin Abdullah bin Abdulrahman Al Saud, and organisations in Saudi Arabia for sponsoring this exhibition.

Flat-racing and equestrian events in the United Kingdom have for centuries enjoyed royal support and patronage. HM Queen Elizabeth II has continued this royal tradition with evident enthusiasm and pleasure. This exhibition is offered as a tribute to Her Majesty on the occasion of her Diamond Jubilee.

NEIL MACGREGOR
Director, British Museum

List of lenders

Apart from the British Museum, the objects included in the exhibition *The Horse: from Arabia to Royal Ascot* have been kindly loaned by a number of private and public collections and institutions. The British Museum would like to thank all the lenders for their generosity.

Kingdom of Saudi Arabia

King Abdulaziz Public Library, Riyadh
King Saud University Museum, Riyadh
Layan Cultural Foundation, Jeddah
National Museum of Saudi Arabia, Riyadh

United Kingdom

British Library, London
Fitzwilliam Museum, Cambridge
Jockey Club Estates, Newmarket
Royal Armouries
Royal Collection
Tate, London

Switzerland

Olympic Museum, Lausanne

Individual lenders

HRH Prince Khalid Abdullah
Mrs A.A. Edmunds
Nicholas Knowles
Richard Meade
Peter Upton

Authors' preface and acknowledgements

THE HORSE has played a hugely important part in human history. From its domestication around five and a half thousand years ago, somewhere in the grassy steppe lands that stretch from the Danube to the Altai Mountains, up until modern times, the horse has been an essential element in many of the world's major cultures. Until the age of mechanization, even within living memory, horses were essential for transport, either ridden or pulling vehicles, in warfare, and in industry. Only recently has the emphasis shifted to recreational and sporting activities, including flat-racing, steeple chasing, and equestrianism. In a single exhibition, it would be quite impossible to cover all aspects of the history of the horse, embracing all areas and all periods. We have therefore had to be selective, and this exhibition and accompanying book focus on the Middle East, which is in itself a key area for the development of horses, and describe how oriental horses were brought into Britain from the early seventeenth century onwards and were bred with native British and Irish mares to produce the Thoroughbred horse. An important link in this story is the Arabian horse, in that all modern Thoroughbreds trace their lineage back to two or three Arabian sires, but there were of course in antiquity and still are today many other types of horse in the Middle East. In fact, the further one goes back in time the more difficult it is to recognize particular breeds of horse, and at best one can only point to resemblances to modern breeds. It is not until a relatively late date that one can talk with confidence about particular breeds. The exhibition, then, first looks at the history of the horse in the Middle East from ancient times until the modern period, to see the context from which oriental horses including the Arabian horse emerged. We then look at the evidence for the horse in the Arabian Peninsula, which gives us the opportunity to introduce the GigaPan project. This is an innovative photographic survey of rock drawings featuring horses that will be presented for the first time during the exhibition. Two important individuals in the importation of oriental horses into Britain, although they were active at a time when the Thoroughbred breed had already been established, were Lady Anne Blunt and her husband Wilfrid Scawen Blunt. Nowadays, the Crabbet Stud that they established in Sussex is renowned for its role in preserving the purebred Arabian horse. In Britain, much effort was put into improving the stock of native

horses, and by the eighteenth century the Thoroughbred had emerged. The exhibition finishes with a review of modern horse racing, which is restricted to Thoroughbreds, but also touches on modern equestrian events such as the Olympics where the competing horses are not Thoroughbreds but may have the blood of Oriental horses in their veins. Lastly, we point to the continuing story of the pure Arabian horse, which is bred, admired and appreciated around the world, and often takes part in events such as endurance racing, in which it excels.

The British Museum has long wanted to present an exhibition on the horse, and in part this exhibition had its genesis in the two wonderful volumes on Furusiyya (Horsemanship) prepared for the press by David Alexander and published in Riyadh in 1996. These volumes were intended to accompany a large exhibition in Riyadh which in the end did not materialize, but the seeds were sown for a major international exhibition on the horse. Such an exhibition was eventually mounted in the International Museum of the Horse in Kentucky Horse Park in the summer of 2010, under the title *A Gift from the Desert: the Art, History and Culture of the Arabian Horse*. We are most grateful to the curators of this exhibition, Sandra Olsen and Cynthia Culbertson, and the Director of the Museum of the Horse, Bill Cooke, for sharing some ideas with us, and some of the objects shown in Kentucky are included in the present exhibition, but inevitably the end-products are very different.

The core curatorial team has been John Curtis, who was Keeper of the Middle East Department in the British Museum 1989–2011, and is now Keeper of Special Middle East Projects, Nigel Tallis, who is Curator of the Assyrian Collection in the British Museum, and Astrid Johansen, who has been Project Curator for the exhibition since 1 October 2011. Others who have been particularly closely involved in the preparation of the exhibition are Robert Frith (Designer), Claire Edwards (Interpretation Officer), Matt Big (2D designer), Maria Blyzinsky (Project Manager) and Alex Lawson (Development). This group is very grateful to Neil MacGregor and Andrew Burnett of the British Museum Directorate, Joanna Mackle (Director of Public Engagement), Carolyn Marsden Smith (Head of Exhibitions), and Jonathan Tubb (Keeper of the Middle East Department) for their help and support. Other colleagues in the British Museum who have given freely of their expertise, advice and assistance include Ladan Akbarnia, Fahmida Suleman, St John Simpson, Venetia Porter, Sarah Choy and Jane Newson (Middle East), Hugo Chapman and Sheila O'Connell (Prints and Drawings), Neal Spencer (Ancient Egypt and Sudan), Philip Attwood, Thomas Hockenhull and Vesta Sarkhosh Curtis (Coins and Medals), Chris Spring (Africa, Oceania and the Americas), Judith Swaddling (Greek and Roman), Karen Birkhoelzer and Alice Rugheimer (Conservation and Scientific Research), Michael Row and Ivor Kerslake (Photography), David McNeff (Loans Manager), Hannah Payne, Caroline Ingham and Sian Flynn (Exhibitions), Stuart Frost (Head of Interpretation), Hannah Boulton (Communications), Jessica Hunt, Sonia D'Orsi and Ann Lumley (Marketing), Sukie Hemming, Jemma Jones and Clare Tomlinson (Development), and Rosemary Bradley, Roderick Buchanan, Kate Horwood, Angela Pountney, Axelle Russo, Holly Smith and Susan Walby (British Museum Company).

In order to keep this exhibition within manageable proportions, it was decided at the outset to limit the display to objects from the British Museum's own very rich collection supplemented by loans from Saudi Arabia and from various institutions and individuals in the United Kingdom. This we have done, with one exception, a poster from the Olympic Museum in Lausanne. We are extremely grateful to all lenders whose generosity has meant that we have we have been able to assemble such a varied and interesting exhibition. After the names of the lending institutions the names are given in brackets of those who facilitated the loans: the Saudi Commission for Tourism and Antiquities (Ali I. Al-Ghabban); the King Abdulaziz Public Library (HE Faisal Abdulrahman bin Muaammer, Abdul Kareem Al-Zaid, Fahad Al-Abdulkareem); the King Abdulaziz Arabian Horse Centre at Dirab (Sami Suleiman al-Nohait, Guy Rhodes); the Layan Cultural Foundation, Jeddah (HH Prince Faissal bin Abdullah bin Muhammad al-Saud); the Royal Collection, United Kingdom (Jonathan Marsden); the British Library (Colin Baker and Arnold Hunt); the Fitzwilliam Museum, Cambridge (Tim Potts and David Scrace); the Tate Gallery (Sir Nicholas Serota); the Royal Armouries, Leeds (Thom Richardson); the National Horseracing Museum, Newmarket (Chris Garibaldi and Graham Snelling); the Jockey Club, Newmarket (William Gittus); and the Olympic Museum, Lausanne (Frédérique Jamolli). Thanks are also due to the following individuals who have generously lent us material: HRH Prince Khalid Abdullah, Richard Meade, Nicholas Knowles, Mrs A.A. Edmunds and Peter Upton (who also gave us valuable information about the history of the Arabian horse) and Jila Peacock and Afsoon Hayley for donations of their work.

It is a privilege to be able to include in this exhibition some examples of GigaPan photography, and we are grateful to the Director of the project Richard T. Bryant for making this possible. We should also like to thank Kieran Baker for interesting discussions about the making of a documentary film about the life of Lady Anne Blunt.

We have benefited considerably from the combined wisdom of the Advisory Committee, whose members were Saad al-Rashid, David Alexander, Sandra Olsen and Rachel Ward. Dr Saad in particular has been a tower of strength, encouraging us, monitoring progress, and acting as a bridge between ourselves and colleagues in Saudi Arabia. Other individuals who have given generously of their time and advice and sometimes steered us towards important loans include Catherine Wills, James Swartz, John Roche and Ahmed Moustafa. We have also benefited from the advice of the two owners of Arabian horses in the British Museum, Alice Rugheimer and Elizabeth Pendleton.

In Saudi Arabia Khalid H. Tahir, Hany Ahmed Alshuweir and Wedyan Osama Darandary of NCB Capital did much to progress this exhibition, while in London the staff of the Royal Embassy of Saudi Arabia have been extremely helpful, notably the ambassador HRH Prince Mohammed bin Nawaf bin Abdul Aziz al-Saud, Anne Morris and Jennifer Zulfiqar.

This catalogue has been produced in a relatively short period of time, and the credit for this is entirely due to our editor Coralie Hepburn who has been a model of patience and efficiency. We would also like to thank Ray Watkins who did the layout with great skill at short notice. The catalogue entries for the Islamic period objects and the chapter on the horse in the Islamic world were kindly read by our colleague Ladan Akbarnia, who suggested a few amendments, but any faults that remain are of course the responsibility of the authors.

Lastly, the warmest thanks of all are reserved for HH Prince Faissal bin Abdullah bin Muhammad Al-Saud, whose enthusiasm, vision and generosity have greatly helped to bring about this exhibition.

John Curtis and Nigel Tallis

List of maps

Opposite: The western steppe in relation to early Mesopotamian sites mentioned in the text.

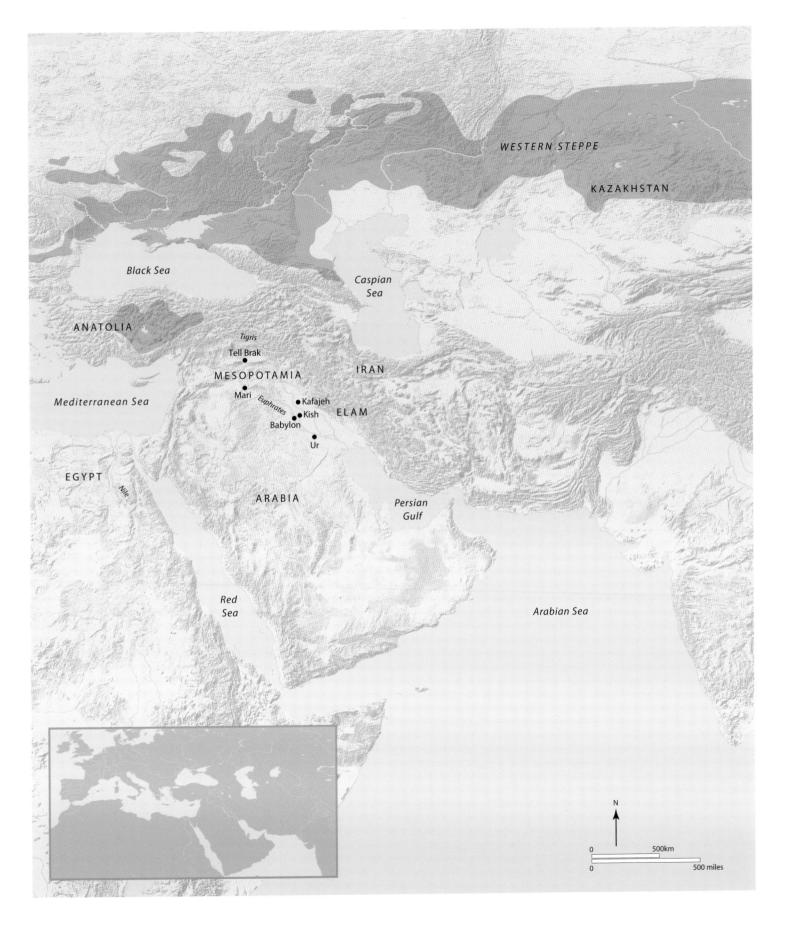

WESTERN STEPPE

KAZAKHSTAN

Black Sea

*Caspian
Sea*

ANATOLIA

Tigris
Tell Brak

MESOPOTAMIA

IRAN

Mediterranean Sea

Mari

Euphrates
Kafajeh
Kish

ELAM

Babylon
Ur

EGYPT

Nile

ARABIA

Persian
Gulf

*Red
Sea*

Arabian Sea

N

0   500km

0   500 miles

CHAPTER I

THE HORSE IN THE ANCIENT NEAR EAST

The horse in the Ancient Near East

ABOVE

Fig. 1

Part of a stone Assyrian wall panel showing a groom leading a pair of horses, c. 710 BC. This relief comes from the Palace of Sargon II at Khorsobad in Assyria (now northern Iraq) and may show tribute being brought to the Assyrian king. The horses wear crescentic crests with elaborate brow cushions and have tassels suspended under their necks.
BM 118828

BEFORE the introduction of the horse, people in the Ancient Near East used donkeys, asses and oxen to pull cumbersome four-wheeled vehicles or sledges. Amongst the earliest depictions of such wheeled vehicles in Western Asia are pictograms on clay tablets from Sumer in southern Mesopotamia, dating from about 3000 BC, which show a roofed cabin mounted on wheels, sometimes with a reed- or basket-work curtain at the side, and with a curved pole or runner at the front. An alternative interpretation is that these are not wheels but numerals indicating numbers of workmen.

The best-known representations of early vehicles, however, are on a so-called 'Standard' found at the Sumerian city of Ur in southern Iraq in a royal cemetery. It dates from around 2600 BC, and is perhaps the sounding box for a musical instrument. It consists of a wooden box covered with bitumen into which is set a mosaic inlay made up of shell and different coloured stones (cat. 1). On one side of the Standard is a scene of farming and banqueting, while on the other is a scene of war. In this representation of a Sumerian army, five war chariots are shown. Each vehicle has a high front to protect the driver, who has a seat, hidden here but visible on clay models, and a platform at the rear on which a man armed with javelins or an axe may stand. The solid wheels are made of

three pieces of wood clamped together. The chariot pole is attached to the base of the car and comes up to the shoulders of the four draft-animals. They are controlled by reins which pass through a rein-ring mounted on the chariot pole above a simple yoke to which the animals were attached with collars. These reins are attached to rings through the upper lips of the animals. The purpose of the nose bands, held in place by headstalls, was probably to muzzle the animals (as shown very clearly on other inlays from Kish and Mari), which are apparently crosses from wild asses or donkeys. A similar animal is shown on an electrum rein-ring from Ur.

Models of chariots and representations of them are known from a number of other sites of this date. For example, at Tell Brak in Syria, a seal and a seal impression of the third millennium BC both show a chariot with four solid wheels being pulled by a team of four equids similar to those on the Standard of Ur. In this case they are probably donkeys because the skeletons of six animals have been found that have been identified as donkeys at the same site. They had been ritually sacrificed around 2200 BC and carefully buried in or near a small temple.

These early vehicles were probably fairly speedy (as confirmed by modern reconstructions) but they were difficult to turn and control, and were probably unstable. The

Fig. 2
The ruler and his entourage followed by his four-wheeled chariot, its team of four asses or donkeys held by a groom, shown on the Standard of Ur, c. 2600 BC (cat. 1).

Fig. 3
Bronze or copper breast band (draught collar) with embossed decoration from the Royal Cemetery at Ur in Mesopotamia, dating from around 2600 BC. This collar was worn by one of two oxen pulling a ceremonial sledge. Part of the jaw-bone of the ox is still attached to the collar. Two copper toggles are preserved at each end of the almost intact collar so that it could be fastened to the yoke. The earliest harness collars for asses and horses were based on ox harness.
BM 121480

animals must also have been difficult to handle. Directional control of the team was through a goad (spiked stick) and braking was by reins attached to the nose-ring. The introduction of bits, even for donkeys, was rather later. The earliest certain evidence for the use of a bit in the Middle East is from Tel Haror in Israel, where a donkey skeleton complete with bronze bit has been found in a Middle Bronze Age context (c. 1700 BC). There is possibly earlier evidence for metal bits from Tell Brak, but this is as yet inconclusive.

Horses were probably not introduced into the Ancient Near East in any quantity until about 2000 BC, after they had been first domesticated elsewhere. Exactly where and when wild horses were first domesticated is hotly disputed, but it seems likely that it was somewhere on the grassy plains known as the Eurasian steppes that stretch from Eastern Europe to Mongolia, which provided ideal pasture for herds of wild horses. These types of wild horse included the breed known as Przewalski's horse, but these have never been domesticated. Dr Sandra Olsen, Curator of Anthropology at the Carnegie Museum of Natural History in Pittsburgh, Pennsylvania, has argued plausibly that horses were first domesticated in the Botai culture of northern Kazakhstan in about 3500 BC. This is based on findings in archaeological excavations in which she took part in Kazakhstan between 1994 and 2002. The evidence for domestication includes leg bones thinner than those of wild horses and markings on the teeth of horse skeletons showing they had been bridled. Whatever the precise details may have been, there is no doubt that, in the words of Lord Colin Renfrew, 'the domestication of the horse was one of the most significant events in the development of many human societies, ushering in new modes of transport and warfare and generating social and political change'. Other important developments have been linked to the domestication of the horse, such as the spread of wheeled vehicles and even the spread of Indo-European languages, but while cogent arguments have been put forward for these theories they remain unproven at present.

The earliest certain evidence for horses in the Ancient Near East shows them being ridden. For example, there is a Mesopotamian terracotta plaque in the British Museum dating from about 1750 BC that shows a horse with a long hairy tail, possibly exaggerated to show it is not a donkey's tail, being ridden by a man who controls it with reins and a stick. He rides it as one would ride a donkey, far back on the rump, and has no saddle and no stirrups but instead uses a strap around the horse's belly to help keep his seat. However, at this early date horses, nearly always stallions, were mostly used as harness animals in teams of two for pulling chariots. In Mesopotamia and later in Egypt the introduction of the horse led to the development of light, fast chariots with two spoked wheels. From about 1600 BC there was a sweeping change in the nature of warfare and the use of the horse in the Ancient Near East. The fast chariot, which had been known for some two hundred years, now finally reached its full military potential, ushering in what is often known as 'the chariot age'. This came about through the introduction of full defensive armour for horse, vehicle and crew and a complete offensive armament for mounted and foot combat (a powerful composite bow, a large number of arrows, javelins, hand weapons and thrusting spears). Provided and maintained under royal patronage by a military aristocracy, the concept of the 'chariot-system' was to reign supreme throughout the Near East for nearly 1000 years and in modified form was to spread into the Bronze Age Aegean states, India and China. These developments largely came about through a highland people known as the Hurrians, who during the second millennium BC began to form a growing element in the populations of Syria and northern Mesopotamia. By the seventeenth century BC several Hurrian states had formed in these regions and within the following century a confederation of these states between the Euphrates and Tigris, known as the kingdom of Mitanni, had established control over most of Syria and northern Mesopotamia. The skills of horsemanship and chariot warfare were particularly associated with the Hurrians and a high-status class of warriors called 'mariannu'. The influence on contemporary peoples of the Hurrians in equestrian and military matters extended to the powerful Hittites whose capital was at Boğazköy in central Turkey. There are a number of Hittite texts in cuneiform dealing with the training of horses, the best-known of which is the Kikkuli text. This is a chariot horse-training text written in the Hittite language and originally dating from the fifteenth century. It begins: 'thus speaks Kikkuli, master horse trainer of the land of Mitanni.' Pressured by both Egypt, the Hittites and then by Assyria, the kingdom of Mitanni finally collapsed in the thirteenth century BC, but Hurri-Mitannian influence on army organization and equipment was all-pervasive and can be seen in all the Near Eastern states for which we have evidence, from New

Fig. 4
Egyptian wall painting from the tomb of Nebamun at Thebes, c. 1500 BC, showing the assessment of crops to establish the payment of tax. Five vertical registers of hieroglyphs on the left side survive. The centre of the fragment is divided into two registers with chariots shown in civil use: the upper register depicts a chariot with a team of two horses, one black and one chestnut, held by the driver, while the lower register shows an indentical chariot drawn by a pair of asses or hinnies with the driver resting in the vehicle. The horses are shown with high tail carriages and arched necks, features that are also present in the later Arabian horse (see cat. 11).
BM 37982

Kingdom Egypt to the Hittites (and even Bronze Age Greece), to the Middle-Assyrian kingdom and Kassite Babylonia.

Horses were much prized, and they were often given as diplomatic gifts in the later second millennium BC, as seen in the Amarna letters. The letters from this archive of royal correspondence with neighbouring kings, found in Egypt but written in the diplomatic language of Babylonian cuneiform, usually begin with an official statement of good wishes for the ruler's 'household, your wives, your sons, your country, your magnates, your horses, your chariots', and commonly include the description of kingly gifts, including five teams of horses from Burnaburiash of Babylon to Amenophis IV or Tutankhamun of Egypt, and long inventories of gifts of horses 'that run swiftly', chariots, harness and equipment, '1 set of bridles, their blinkers of ivory'. It is also in the art of this time, especially in Egyptian tomb-paintings, that we can first see horses with characteristics we now most closely associate with the Arabian breed we know today: for example, a high-arched tail, a short back and prominent eyes.

According to the Bible, Solomon owned a large number of horses. Thus we read in the Book of Chronicles (2 Chronicles 9, v. 25): 'And Solomon had four thousand stalls for horses and chariots, and twelve thousand horsemen, whom he stationed in the chariot cities and with the king in Jerusalem.' We are also told that the horses came from Egypt and Ku'e (possibly Adana in Turkey), and that Solomon's traders also acted as middlemen: 'And Solomon's import of horses was from Egypt and Ku'e, and the king's traders received them from Ku'e for a price. They imported a chariot from Egypt for six hundred shekels of silver, and a horse for a hundred and fifty; likewise through them these were exported to all the kings of the Hittites and the kings of Syria' (2 Chronicles 1, vv. 16–17).

Around 1000 BC horse riding became more widespread, particularly in areas which were suitable for breeding horses. Nowhere was this more evident than the Luristan region of western Iran, where between 1000 and 700 BC there was a thriving culture, perhaps semi-nomadic, which was clearly very dependent on horses. The Luristan culture is renowned for the fine bronze castings that it produced, very often in the form of horse harness and trappings. Many of these have been discovered in the graves of warriors who were buried not only with a set of weapons abut also with a set of horse harness. It seems that horse-bits with associated cheekpieces, the latter often very elaborate, were often placed under the head of the corpse like a pillow.

From their homeland on the River Tigris in northern Iraq, Assyrian armies campaigned widely in the Ancient Near East between about 900 BC and 612 BC. The horses that were needed for this expansion had to be obtained from abroad, as the barren uplands of Assyria were scarcely suitable for raising them. The highland areas to the north and east of Assyria – Urartu, Mannaea and Media – were particularly rich sources. The lush grasslands of the Zagros foothills and the Iranian plateau were ideal breeding grounds. Horses are often listed in the annals of the Assyrian kings among the prizes of war, but they were not only imported as military booty. For example, cuneiform tablets from both Nineveh and Nimrud known as 'horse reports' show that horses were brought to Assyria peaceably from many different parts of the Ancient Near East. Most deliveries were made in the spring, just before the campaign season. Large 'Kushite' chariot horses were even brought from distant Nubia.

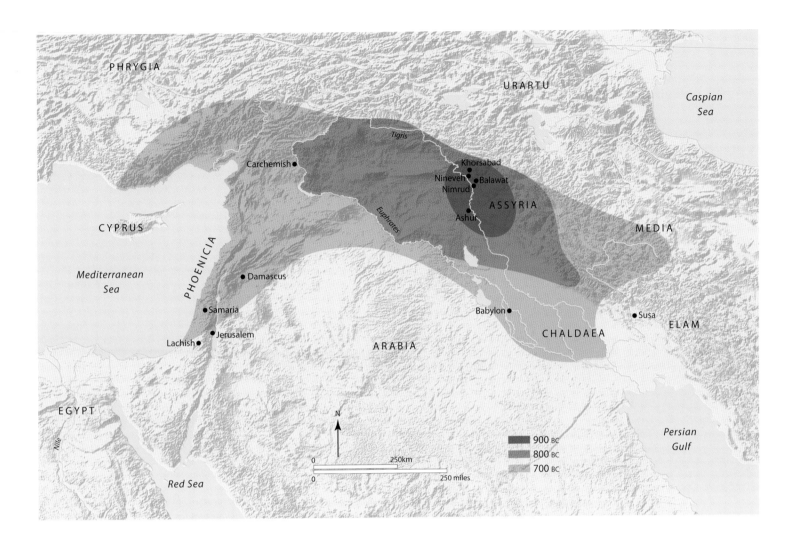

Map labels:

PHRYGIA · URARTU · Caspian Sea · Tigris · Carchemish · Khorsabad · Nineveh · Balawat · Nimrud · ASSYRIA · MEDIA · CYPRUS · Euphrates · Ashur · Mediterranean Sea · PHOENICIA · Damascus · Babylon · Susa · ELAM · Samaria · CHALDAEA · Jerusalem · Lachish · ARABIA · EGYPT · Nile · N · Persian Gulf · Red Sea

0 250km
0 250 miles

900 BC
800 BC
700 BC

Information about horses and horse trappings comes from contemporary cunei-form texts, the stone reliefs lining the walls of Assyrian palaces, and objects found in ex-cavations at Assyrian sites. Horse bits were made from iron or bronze, and blinkers and nose guards were made of bronze or ivory. Leather bridles and harness straps were deco-rated with ornaments in bronze, ivory, shell and stone. Some of the elaborate carved ivory harness elements, particularly blinkers and frontlets, were imported from Syria and Phoenicia.

From this evidence a broad picture can be built about the role of the horse in an-cient Assyria. Horses were mainly used for pulling chariots in warfare and for hunting dan-gerous or fast game, particularly lions and bulls. Chariot design and equipment, almost unchanged for nearly 1000 years, evolved rapidly between 900 and 700 BC. During this time chariots became bigger, with the number of horses in the team increased from two to three and finally four, and the number of men they could accommodate increased from two to four. With improved riding skills horse riding itself gradually became more commonplace. Mounted troops were mentioned in texts as early as the reign of Tukulti-Ninurta II (890–884 BC) and they are shown on reliefs in the reign of his son Ashurnasirpal II (883–859 BC) and on decorative gate fittings from his palaces at Nimrud and Balawat.

Fig. 5
The expansion of the Assyrian empire
between about 900 and 700 BC.

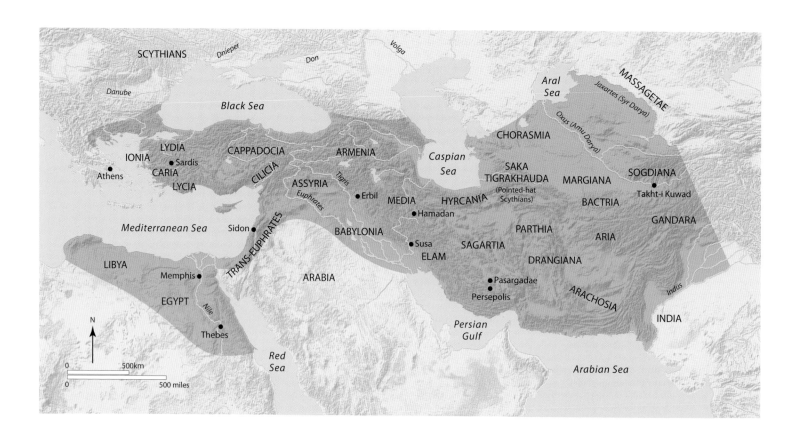

Fig. 6
The Persian empire in the time of
Darius (522–486 BC) showing the
principal provinces.

During this period the cavalry rode in pairs, with one soldier controlling both horses, leaving the other free to use his bow, acting as a chariot crew but without a chariot. Later, soldiers were able to control their own mounts while fighting with bows and spears at the same time. In the detailed report of the eighth campaign of Sargon II (721–705 BC) it is stated that a cavalry unit, one thousand strong, was always stationed by the side of the king. Increasingly large numbers of cavalry are recorded in Assyrian inscriptions, and by around 650 BC we see for the first time cavalry horses with full armour. Previously only chariot horses had been armoured. Even kings now rode on horses, so that by the time of Ashurbanipal (668–631 BC) the king is celebrated as a master of horsemanship in his hunting reliefs.

The horses seem to have increased in size during the Assyrian period, or at least they are shown as larger, more robust animals, probably because stronger animals were needed as chariot crews increased and cavalry became more heavily armed. There is no appreciable difference between cavalry and draft horses, except in details of harness.

The contemporary kingdom of Urartu, occupying the mountainous areas to the north of Assyria, was also famous for its use of horses, and many splendid bronze horse trappings are associated with this civilization.

Between 539 BC and 331 BC the whole of the Ancient Near East was brought under the control of a Persian dynasty known as the Achaemenids. Horses were an important part of their culture. The Greek historian Herodotus (c. 484–425 BC) wrote in his *Histories* that 'the Persians teach their sons, between the ages of five and twenty, only three things: to ride a horse, use a bow and speak the truth.' Darius, one of the greatest of the Achaemenid kings (522–486 BC), recorded in a monumental inscription in the Old Persian language, 'Trained am I both with hands and with feet. As a horseman I am a good horseman. As a bowman I am a good bowman both afoot and on horseback. As a spearman I am a good spearman both afoot and on horseback'.[1] The Persian empire stretched from North Africa to the Indus Valley and from the Caucasus to the Persian Gulf, and to administer this vast area good transport communications were essential. The so-called Royal Road extended from Sardis in Eastern Turkey to Susa in south-west Iran and depended on a system of post horses. Horses were also widely used in the wars with Greece (490–479 BC). The main breed of horse used both for riding and pulling chariots were the 'Great Nisaean' horses said by classical authors to have been bred on the plains of Media in Iran. In addition to these, however, the stone reliefs at the Persian capital of Persepolis show horses being presented to the Persian king by subject peoples from around the empire. The north and east sides of the Apadana Palace which are mirror images of each other show twenty-three delegations bringing presents to the great king. Horses (in all cases stallions) are being brought by six delegations, namely the Armenians, the Cappadocians, the 'pointed-hat' Scythians, the Sagartians, the hauma-venerating Scythians and the European Scythians. It is interesting that all the members of these delegations wear trouser-suits, partly reflecting the Iranian origins of some, but also underlining the clear association of the wearing of trousers with the riding of horses. In

Fig. 7
Detail from a plaster cast made of the Apadana reliefs at Persepolis by the Weld-Blundell expedition in 1892 showing part of a delegation from Cappadocia (central Turkey) bringing a stallion and Median robes as presents for the king of Persia, 5th century BC. This powerful and stocky horse has its forelock tied into a splayed tuft, with long strands of mane arranged on the shoulder and the tail tied in a mud knot – all typical Achaemenid Persian features, as are the details of harness. In some cases these casts now preserve more detail than the originals.
BM C.228.3

Fig. 8
The Alexander Mosaic was found in
the House of the Faun in Pompeii, Italy,
and dates from the Ist century BC.
It is thought to be copy of a fourth-
century BC painting, and probably
shows the Battle of Issus in 333 BC.
Alexander is shown on horseback on
the far left, while Darius III is riding in a
two-wheeled chariot in the centre. The
chariot is pulled by four black horses
and the chariot driver holds the reins in
one hand and a whip in the other. The
artist, perhaps not knowing Persian
harness, has shown Greek bits and
harness fittings.
National Archaeological Museum,
Naples

addition to the individual horses, horse-drawn chariots are being brought by the Lydians
and the Libyans. The Indian delegation brings a donkey. The fact that two delegations
bring chariots shows that they were by no means obsolete by this time, but continued as
high-status civil vehicles, and this is confirmed by the archaeological record.

The Persepolis reliefs show two-wheeled royal chariots that are especially for the
use of the king, and these chariots are of similar design to the model gold chariot in the
Oxus Treasure (see cat. 98). The horses pulling the Oxus Treasure chariot are surprisingly
small, which has led to suggestions that they might be Caspian horses. This is a breed that
was thought to have died out until it was rediscovered in northern Iran in the 1960s by a
horse breeder called Louise Firouz. The Caspian is characterized by its small size (11.2
hands at the withers), high work-rate, jumping ability and intelligence. It is certain that in
antiquity and in the following Islamic period there were a number of different breeds of horse,
and some or all of them may be related to what subsequently came to be called the Arabian.

As well as for ceremonial purposes chariots were also used on occasion in battle,
in specialized form in limited numbers as a terror weapon with blades and scythes, and as
command vehicles. Thus, the last Persian king, Darius III (336–331 BC), is shown in a chariot in the so-called Alexander Mosaic from a house in Pompeii, which depicts a battle
between Alexander's forces and those of the Persians, probably at Issus in 333 BC. Darius
is shown in a chariot, while Alexander is shown on his horse Bucephalus.

From around 250 BC onwards the Ancient Near East was invaded by a tribe of
Iranian nomads known as the Parthians. They were skilled horsemen and wore trousers,

often with the addition of leggings, to facilitate their life in the saddle. The Roman historian Justin, summarizing an earlier work by Pompeius Trogus, wrote that the Parthians 'ride on horseback on all occasions; on horses they go to war, and to feasts; on horses they discharge public and private duties; on horses they go abroad, meet together, traffic, and converse.'[2] The rise to power of the Parthians, and the consolidation of their hold over Iran and Mesopotamia, brought them into conflict with Rome, which was expanding eastwards. They proved to be a powerful adversary for Rome. In his *Roman History* the Latin historian Cassius Dio recorded: 'They are really formidable in warfare (and) even to this day they hold their own in the wars they wage against us ... The Parthians make no use of a shield, but their forces consist of mounted archers and pikemen [lancers], mostly in full armour. Their infantry is small, made up of the weaker men; but even these are all archers. They practise from boyhood, and the climate and the land combine to aid both horsemanship and archery. The land, being for the most part level, is excellent for raising horses and very suitable for riding about on horseback; at any rate, even in war they lead about whole droves of horses, so that they can use different ones at different times, can ride up suddenly from a distance and also retire to a distance speedily; and the atmosphere there, which is very dry and does not contain the least moisture, keeps their bowstrings tense, except in the dead of winter.'[3] In *Antony and Cleopatra*, Shakespeare refers to 'the ne'er-yet-beaten horse of Parthia'.

The main encounter with Rome occurred in 53 BC at the Battle of Carrhae (modern Harran in Turkey) when a force led by Crassus was roundly defeated. On this occasion the light Parthian archers, shooting from horseback, supporting the completely armoured lancers, carried all before them. We know from classical authors that their victory was

Fig. 9
The Parthian and Sasanian empires.

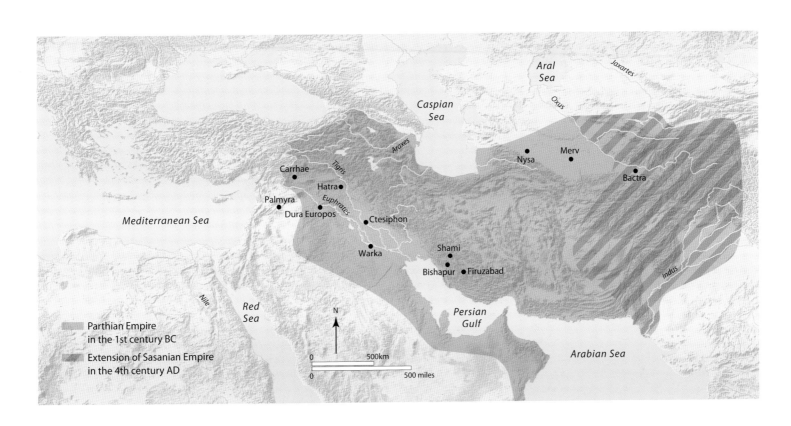

Mediterranean Sea

Aral Sea

Jaxartes

Caspian Sea

Oxus

Araxes

Tigris

Merv

Nysa

Bactra

Carrhae

Hatra

Euphrates

Palmyra

Dura Europos

Ctesiphon

Shami

Warka

Bishapur • Firuzabad

Nile

Red Sea

N

Persian Gulf

Indus

Arabian Sea

Parthian Empire
in the 1st century BC

Extension of Sasanian Empire
in the 4th century AD

0   500km

0   500 miles

Fig. 10
Rock carving on the back wall of a
grotto at Taq-i Bustan, Iran, showing
the Sasanian king Khusrow II (Parviz)
(AD 591–628) on horseback. Both king
and horse are heavily armoured. The
side walls of the grotto show a boar
hunt and a deer hunt respectively.

partly due to their tactic of shooting backwards from horseback, much feared by the Romans and known as 'the Parthian shot'. This method of fighting is described by both Plutarch and Justin. In his *Life of Crassus*, Plutarch tells us that 'the Parthians threw their darts as they fled, an art in which none but the Scythians exceed them, and it is, indeed, a cunning practice, for while they thus fight to make their escape, they avoid the dishonour of a flight'.[4] According to Justin, 'They fight on horseback, either galloping forward or turning their backs. Often, too, they counterfeit flight, that they may throw their pursuers off their guard against being wounded by their arrows ... In general they retire before the enemy in the very heat of the engagement, and, soon after their retreat, return to the battle afresh; so that, when you feel most certain that you have conquered them, you have still to meet the greatest danger from them. Their armour, and that of their horses, is formed of plates, lapping over one another like the feathers of a bird, and covers both man and horse entirely.'[5]

Some authorities have seen a connection between the Parthian horses and the Arabian horse, but this remains unproven. From the first century AD onwards, by which time the Parthians had become prosperous, there are a number of rock reliefs showing scenes of jousting, a tradition that continued in later periods. In AD 224 the Parthians were replaced by another Iranian dynasty known as the Sasanians, who ruled until the Islamic conquest. In Zoroastrianism, which became the state religion in the Sasanian period, the horse is classed as 'ass-hoofed' (xarpay), one of the beneficent grazing animals. It is also associated with the sun – Mithra – and a chariot pulled by horses. The horse is also one of the three forms of the god Tishtrya (the star Sirius). Sasanian kings hunted lions and other animals on horseback, often apparently in special hunting parks or 'paradise' gardens. The jousting contests known from the Parthian period now became very popular and are shown on a number of Sasanian rock reliefs as symbols of victory. The heavily armoured horses and riders are the forerunners of the European knights of the Middle Ages.

Probably the best known example of an armoured Sasanian warrior on horseback is the stone carving in high relief of the king identified as Khusrow Parviz (the 'victorious') (AD 591–628) at the back of a grotto at Taq-i Bustan near Kermanshah in Iran. The king wears a coat of mail, a helmet with mail face covering, and a quiver, and he carries a shield and a long lance. His horse is also heavily protected, with a coat of armour covering his neck and chest. He sits on a saddle with raised back and sides which stopped him from falling off the horse while fighting. It is usually thought this horse was the famous Shabdiz (meaning 'the colour of night') who featured in later literary epics. In Nizami's *Khusrow and Shirin*, Shabdiz takes Shirin to Khusrow after she has fallen in love with his portrait, and in the Iranian Book of Kings (*Shahnameh*) the minstrel Barbad informs Khusrow of the death of Shabdiz through a song, thereby risking his own life.

Khusrow II is shown without stirrups, as are other Sasanian kings on their rock reliefs, which lends support to the view that rigid stirrups were not introduced into the Ancient Near East until the Islamic period (see below). However, before this time soft stirrups and hook stirrups seem to have been widely known. They were probably intended to be mounting aids for poor riders or the infirm.

CHAPTER 2

THE HORSE IN THE ISLAMIC WORLD

The horse in the Islamic world

Fig. 11
Illustration from the *Furusiyya*
manuscript dating from 773 AH/AD 1371
(cat. 134) showing a rider on a red horse
brandishing two swords and captioned
'Illustration of a horseman with a sword
in his right hand, its blade on his left
shoulder and a sword in his left hand
whose blade is under his right armpit.'
British Library

Fig. 12
Mughal miniature painting from
c. AD 1790 showing the lovers Baz Bahadur
(the last Sultan of Malwa) and Rupmati
riding horses by moonlight. Both horses,
one dapple-grey and one chestnut, have
their lower legs decorated with henna.
BM 1913,0617.0.3

THE ISLAMIC conquests in the seventh century AD ushered in religious, political, and social change, a gradual process that was to last several centuries. However, a degree of religious and cultural cohesion was given to a much wider area than before, extending eventually to Spain and into Central Asia, and the seventh century therefore serves as a convenient period in which to introduce a break in our story.

Although in the early stages of the Islamic conquest horses may not have been very plentiful, their worth and value were certainly recognized and they were much prized, indeed by Muhammad himself. This is clear from the references to horses in the Quran where they are referred to as gifts of Allah, and splendid horses are listed among the comforts of life on earth. Thus we read 'He [Allah] has given you horses, mules, and donkeys, which you may ride or use as ornaments; and he has created other things beyond your knowledge' (16.8), and 'splendid horses' are among the comforts of this life (3:14). Horses were also important in spreading the word of the Prophet: 'Let the unbelievers not think that they will escape us. They have not the power to do so. Muster against them all the men and cavalry at your disposal, so that you may strike terror into the enemies of Allah and the faithful, and others beside them' (8:60). They were also

apparently crucial in the intertribal warfare that was prevalent in Arabia before and during the lifetime of Muhammad. Reference is made to 'the snorting war steeds, which strike fire with their hoofs as they gallop to the raid at dawn and with a trail of dust split the foe in two' (100:1–6). Horses had also been important in the time of King Solomon: 'He [Solomon] was a good and faithful servant. When, one evening, his prancing steeds were ranged before him, he said: "My love for the good things of life has caused me to forget my prayers; for now the sun has vanished behind the veil of darkness. Bring me back my chargers!" [after the evening prayers are completed]. And with this he fell to hacking [stroking] their legs and necks' (38:27). There are further indications of the importance of horses in the Hadith, the sayings and beliefs that were attributed to Muhammad and were gathered during the eighth and ninth centuries AD. Thus we are told that horses are kept for three reasons. They may be a source of reward for one man, a 'shelter' (that is, a means of earning money) for another, and a burden (a source of sins against Islam) for a third. The man for whom the horse is a source of reward keeps it for Allah's cause (*Jihad*), and when he tethers the horse in a meadow he will get a reward equal to what it is able to eat and drink.[1] As a special tribute to horses trained for Jihad, Muhammad also said while arranging the forelock of a horse that their forelocks would be blessed until the Day of Judgment.[2] Those who used horses for Jihad were entitled to a larger share of war booty.[3] Last, but by no means least, it was incumbent on everybody, including the Prophet himself, to take good care of horses.[4]

Then also in Islamic tradition there is Buraq (Arabic 'lightning'), the white horse-like creature that transported Muhammad to heaven. It had wings, and was half-mule and half-donkey. It carried Muhammad on his night journey from Mecca to Jerusalem and

Fig. 13
Map of the Islamic world in the tenth century AD.

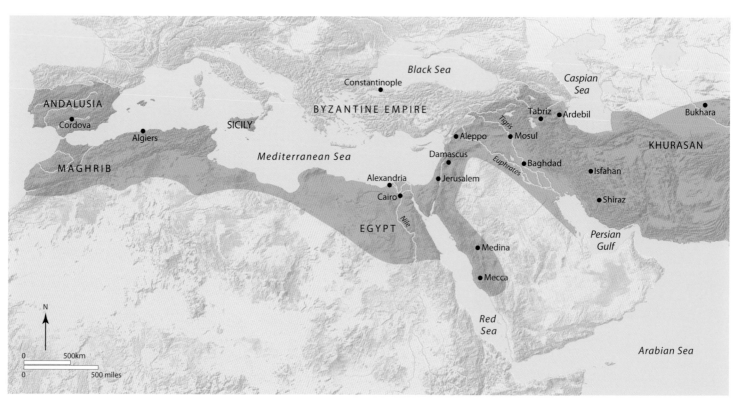

CHAPTER 3

THE HORSE IN ARABIA

The origins of the Arabian breed of horse are not clear. Modern breeds of horses are creations of sometimes many hundreds of years of human intervention. Breeds will therefore change over time, either because of such intervention, or the lack of it, or even vanish completely as human requirements and needs change. Today, the Arabian horse has special characteristics of speed and hardiness but above all of stamina, endurance and temperament. The Arabian breed has a unique and easily recognizable appearance, or conformation, in the shape of the head (with a dished nose and large eyes) and a high arched bearing of the tail. As has been mentioned in earlier chapters, similar physical characteristics are clear in some ancient representations of horses, particularly, for example, in Ancient Egyptian art, while Roman and Byzantine texts describing Arab horsemen often stress the speed and agility of their horses, characteristics which would have been essential for the fluid *karr wa farr* or 'hit and run' warfare which was their speciality.

We see this in the history of Ammianus Marcellinus, a military bureaucrat in the Late Roman administration writing in the fourth century AD. Writing of the *saraceni*, the 'Saracens', Arab warriors who played a major role in the affairs of the Roman East, he says:

> all the men are warriors of equal rank; half naked, clad in coloured cloaks down to the waist, overrunning different countries, with the aid of swift and active horses and speedy camels, alike in times of peace and war.[2]

Ammianus takes most of this digression almost word for word from much earlier authors, but his comment on the speed and agility of Arab horses can be compared with other accounts to show that this at least was probably based on experience rather than literary cliché alone. It is from the close observation of later Byzantine writers that we can most clearly see what was perceived to be the special virtues of Arab horses. The Byzantine emperor Leo VI (886–912), whose compendium on military tactics, the *Taktika* (which, in Arabic translation, was by far the favourite military manual in the Islamic world), noted that Arab Bedouin horses were better than the Byzantine's own. Leo advised that in battle his archers should target the Arab horses,

> for in this manner, with their horses, the so-called *pharia*, being shot at ... they will quickly rush off in flight. They will do this for two reasons, namely because of their desire to save their horses, which are highly prized, and not easily procured, and because they want to save themselves as well through saving the horses.[3]

The word *pharia* is of course clearly derived from *faris*, the Arabic for horse (and in western Europe at the same time we similarly find *alfaraces* is used in Latin texts to describe horses captured from the Arabs in Spain). The Byzantine emperor Nikephoros Phokas (963–969) described in detail in his own book of military tactics the remarkable speed of Arab horses and the impossibility of catching them in pursuit:

> The *Arabitai* [Bedouin] will encircle our four-sided [square] formation in a swarm, as they usually do, confident in their horses. There is no need for the

Fig. 24
Photograph by Abdullatif al-Obaida of a modern Arabian horse showing its characteristic profile. The dished face, large eyes and curled ear-tips typical of the breed are clearly visible.

[Byzantine] cavalry to head off in pursuit of them because of the speed of their horses, for when pursued they are not overtaken and, aided by the speed of their horses, they quickly counterattack and strike against our men. It does no good at all to go chasing after them.[4]

A century later, another Byzantine commentator described the Bedouin 'emboldened as ever by the ability of their horses to run very quickly', but notes significantly, given that modern Arabians are above all known for their endurance, that 'although the Arab horses can run very swiftly for a time, they do not bear up well over a long distance'.[5]

Of course, not keeping a regular formation would give the Bedouin horsemen a speed advantage over the Byzantines, whose military doctrine stressed a steady advance, keeping formation and battle discipline, and Byzantine horses may have been selected for stamina over speed alone, but there is clearly agreement in all these texts that the Arab horses were fast and nimble. Indeed, the Byzantines attributed these remarkable advantages specifically to the horses of Arab semi-nomadic horsemen, something they do not note for any of their other opponents – even other Islamic opponents.

The mythical origins, abilities and training of the Arabian horse were well-established by modern times and the reports of European travellers all agree on the essentials:

> 'Whether it be owing to this extreme care in the breeding, or to the climate which is generally thought favourable, they are certainly very beautiful creatures; although a pure Arabian is seldom of any superior height, yet for docility, form, hardiness, and speed, a rival is difficult to be found. Bred in the tents of the Bedooin, like children, they feed at his hand; and follow their master's steps in his wanderings; or when he falls in battle, remains immovable by his side. With an arched, commanding crest; nervous, straight, compact limbs; the shoulder of a racer, and a spreading open chest; the Arab, when provoked to speed, displays an open nostril that snuffs the wind, an eye of fire, and the action, if not the speed, of the antelope. He scarcely feels the ground, or leaves a print behind; whilst his spirit but seems to rise and display itself with the continuance of the chace [sic] ... The finest [horses] come from the province of Najd, and the Bedooins preserve with a superstitious care the memory and descent of their purest blood; tracing these various breeds to five original sources, which have each given their name to some peculiar race, and are acknowledged as the parent stock. From one or other of these families, the most celebrated Arabians derive their descent through their dam.'[6]

It is said that during the reign of Imam Saud Ibn Abdul Aziz (1803–1814) some 1500 Arabian horses were stabled in al-Dariyah, which was the capital of the first Saudi state (now 20 kilometres from the centre of Riyadh). Al-Dariyah is now a World Heritage Site with a museum on the Arabian horse planned to open in 2013. The gentleness in breaking and training compared to the harshness of European methods was noted by Palgrave, who saw the royal stables of Faisal ibn Saud (1785–1865) at Riyadh on his expedition to Arabia of 1862–3. Palgrave's 'picturesque paragraphs which have since been constantly quoted'

Fig. 25
Photography by Abdullatif al-Obaida of
a modern Arabian horse with tail held
high and flared nostrils.

THE HORSE IN ARABIA

Fig. 26
Sketch by Lady Anne Blunt showing
Arab horsemen on a raid, a loose leaf
from her diary of 16–24 April 1878. This
is the classic pose of the Arab lancer
as captured in rock art, with a long and
flexible cane lance balanced over the
shoulder or held over the head in both
hands. Even in the nineteenth century
the Bedouin horseman disdained the
use of saddle and stirrups (and even
bits, unless absolutely necessary, using
halters as shown here), preferring to
rely on skill and horsemanship.
British Library

(as noted by the Blunts) have often to be treated with caution, but his eyewitness account of Faisal's stables at their height reveal an impressive establishment:

> 'They cover a large square space, about 150 yards each way, and are open in the centre, with a long shed running around the inner walls; under this covering the horses, about 300 in number when I saw them, are picketed during night; in the daytime they may stretch their legs at pleasure within the central courtyard. The greater number are accordingly loose; a few, however, were tied up at their stalls; some, but not many, had horse-cloths over them ... About half the royal stud was present before me, the rest were out at grass, Feysul's entire muster is reckoned at 600 head, or rather more.'[7]

Of Faisal's fine horses, Palgrave thought, 'their appearance justified all reputation, all value, all poetry'. Faisal's territorial ambitions led eventually to his imprisonment in Egypt where he became a friend of the grandson of Muhammad Ali, Abbas Pasha I (1813–1854), the Viceroy of Egypt. Abbas Pasha's greatest passion was the Arabian horse, and he assembled the most famous Arabian stud of the time. The detailed records kept by his representatives of the pedigrees of the horses he acquired, full of vivid anecdotes and histories of their exploits and past owners, forms the unique Abbas Pasha manuscript (cat. 189), which is an essential document for the history of the Arabian breed. Following Abbas Pasha's assassination in 1854, the stud was partly dispersed but Ali Pasha Sherif, the son of the governor of Syria, acquired a significant number of the finest horses.

Johann Ludwig Burckhardt (1784–1817), the Swiss scholar who travelled extensively in the Middle East, noted that 'It is a general but erroneous opinion that Arabia is very rich in horses; but the breed is limited to the extent of fertile pasture-grounds in that country, and it is in such parts only that horses thrive, while those Bedouins who occupy districts of poor soil rarely possess horses. It is found, accordingly, that the tribes most rich in horses are those who dwell in the comparatively fertile plains of Mesopotamia, on the banks of the river Euphrates, and in the Syrian plains. Horses can there feed for several of the spring months upon the green grass and herbs produced by the rains in the valleys and fertile grounds, and such food seems absolutely necessary for promoting the full growth and vigour of the horse. We find that in Najd horses are not nearly so numerous as in the countries before mentioned, and they become scarce in proportion as we proceed towards the south.'[8]

Two generations later, Lady Anne Blunt similarly commented that 'Whatever may have been the case formerly, horses of any kind are now exceedingly rare in Nejd. One may travel vast distances in the peninsula without meeting a single horse, or even crossing a horse-track. Both in the Nefud and on our return journey to the Euphrates, we carefully examined every track of man and beast we met; but . . . not twenty of these proved to be tracks of horses. The wind no doubt obliterates footsteps quickly; but it could not wholly do so, if there were a great number of the animals near. The Ketherin, a true Nejd tribe and a branch of the Bani Khalid, told us with some pride that they could mount a hundred horsemen; and even the Muteyr, reputed to be the greatest breeders of thoroughbred stock in Nejd, are said to possess only 400 mares. The horse is a luxury with the Bedouins of the Peninsula; and not, as it is with those of the north, a necessity of their daily life. Their journeys and raids and wars are all made on camel, not on horseback; and at most the Sheikh mounts his mare at the moment of battle. The want of water in Nejd is a sufficient reason for this. Horses there are kept for show rather than actual use, and are looked upon as far too precious to run unnecessary risks.'[9]

Nowadays, the purity of the Arabian breed is carefully preserved. In the kingdom of Saudi Arabia, for example, all purebred Arabian horses are registered at the King Abdulaziz Arabian Horse Centre at Dirab, 35 kilometres south-west of Riyadh. Each horse is issued with a registration certificate, a passport and a pedigree chart. There are currently nearly 10,000 Arabian horses registered in the Kingdom. The King Abdulaziz Centre is a member of the World Arabian Horse Organization which is concerned with the registration of Arabian horses around the world and has its headquarters in London. The King Abdulaziz Arabian Horse Centre also breeds Arabian horses and there are around 170 horses, comprising stallions, mares and foals there at any one time. King Abdulaziz had a herd of desert-bred warhorses for fighting. These horses typically had larger lungs and stronger bones than European-bred Arabian horses. This unique herd still exists and a number are based at the Centre.

CHAPTER 4

THE ARABIAN HORSE
AND THE BLUNTS

The Arabian horse and the Blunts

Fig. 27
Watercolour sketch by Lady Anne Blunt
showing the 'Pink House' at Sheykh
Obeyd near Cairo in 1900. The Blunts
had this house built in 1891 for the use
of guests, and Lady Anne spent her last
years here from 1906.
British Library

TO-DAY, all day, I rode upon the down,
With hounds and horsemen, a brave company,
On this side in its glory lay the sea,
On that the Sussex weald, a sea of brown.
The wind was light, and brightly the sun shone,
And still we galloped on from gorse to gorse.
And once, when checked, a thrush sang, and my horse
Pricked his quick ears as to a sound unknown.

I knew the spring was come. I knew it even
Better than all by this, that through my chase
In bush and stone and hill and sea and heaven
I seemed to see and follow still your face.
Your face my quarry was. For it I rode,
My horse a thing of wings, myself a god.

St Valentine's Day, Wilfrid Scawen Blunt[1]

Pharaoh.   1881

part of Wilfrid's inheritance following the death of his brother in 1872, and the Blunts had already established a small stud there before they had decided to breed pure Arabians.

Lady Anne kept her own accounts for the estate at Crabbet and her diaries are full of scribbled lists with calculations of feed (oats, hay, bran), straw and shoeing, harness, veterinary bills and labour. Perhaps as was to be expected of the daughter of the brilliant mathematician Ada Lovelace, she calculated every expense – so, in 1877, she noted that each horse or mare cost them seventeen shillings and fourpence-halfpenny per week in upkeep. Her exhaustive summaries of farm expenses included details of every kind, including monthly milk accounts with her pencil notes of consumption of butter cream and milk by dining room, nursery, kitchen, housekeeper's room and servants hall, and purchases of tools and equipment, all carefully itemised in her own hand. Naturally, the same minute attention to detail, essential as her money subsidised Wilfrid, was to be applied to recording the bloodlines of their Arabian horses and it was this which was to prove crucial in establishing the authenticity of the Crabbet stock for the future.

By the end of the year the stud numbered two stallions, nine mares and a foal.

Fig. 32
The dark bay colt Pharaoh with a groom. Pharoah was one of the Blunts' most important early acquisitions, and is shown here in 1881 shortly before his sale and export to Poland the following year.
British Library

Fig. 31
Wilfrid Scawan Blunt in Arab dress with his favourite horse, Sherifa, at Crabbet Park in 1883. Sherifa was a mare from the Nejd, purchased at Aleppo in 1878. Like many of their horses, she bore the scars of battle, in this case the mark of an old spear wound on her near quarter.
British Library

Fig. 33
Modern watercolour painting by
Peter Upton of the grey horse named
Shahwan by the Blunts. This product of
the stud of Ali Pasha Sherif was bought
in 1892. Lady Anne said it was the 'event
of the day and indeed of the winter',
and the horse had the 'unmistakable Ali
Pasha Sherif stamp, so fine in all ways,
beautiful shoulders with excellent
action, tail erect in the air.'

The total cost of the purchase and transport of these first acquisitions was a little less
than £2000. As Lady Anne later wrote:

> My view in having a stud of Arabians that it is a good action to preserve that
> pure blood somewhere else than in Arabia where as time passes it is more and
> more surrounded by dangers, and as to Egypt hitherto breeding has always
> fallen through. Though it need not.

All the initial mares were from the tribes of the Anazeh, except for Sherifa, a Nejd mare
which had belonged to Saud ibn Saud, the emir of Riyadh. The Blunts were rigorous, ruthless in fact, in only breeding from the best of the descendants of their stock and in 1897,
Wilfrid noted that they had preserved descendants from only five of the original mares
of 1877–8 (Queen of Sheba, Basilisk, Dajania, Jerboa and Sherifa).

The Blunts recorded their stock in great detail, and the 'Old Stud List' includes
details of the all-important pedigrees:

Pharaoh bay colt (foaled in 1876) a Seglawi Obeyran of the Ibn Ed Derri purchased from Neddi Ibn Ed Derri of the Resallin (Sebaa Anazeh), his sire a Kehilan Ajuz of the Gomussa (Sebaa Anazeh) his dam's sire a Seqlawi Jedran of Obeyd el Belasi of the Roala (Ruwalla tribe). This strain of blood is considered the best now remaining to the Sebaa.

Pharaoh was one of the most important of the Blunts' early purchases. The transaction was arranged through Skene and made near Palmyra in 1878. The stallion's price was an astonishing £275, reflecting his evident quality. In 1882, when he was six, Pharaoh was sold at the first Crabbet auction when eleven Arabians were sold. He was bought by Count Potocki for 525 guineas, who took him to Poland, and in 1885 Pharoah was sold to the Imperial Russian state stud at Derkoul.

The Blunts' second expedition to the Middle East was to be far more ambitious. This was to the highlands of Nejd in the heart of Arabia itself, said to be the home of the finest Arabian horses and as Wilfrid wrote, 'in the imagination of the Bedouins of the North, is a region of romance, the cradle of their race, and of the ideas of chivalry by which they still live'. They started from Damascus in December 1878 and concluded at Bandar Bushehr in April 1879. At this date the Emir of Hail, Muhammed Ibn Rashid, was paramount in the Nejd and had the finest horses in his stables, many from the stud of Faisal ibn Saud, now displaced as overlord. The winter nights in the desert were cold and the way was hard and unforgiving though ample game of grouse, gazelle and camel gave Wilfrid opportunity to hunt. It was at this point they were attacked by raiders who broke Wilfrid's own gun over his head and struck Lady Anne with a lance before realizing they were under the protection of their ruler. Muhammed Ibn Rashid had a reputation for cold ruthlessness, but the Blunts were well received at Hail as guests of the emir in January 1879. There they stayed several days, finally seeing the famous horses from the royal stud, after some tantalizing delay, with Anne 'almost too excited to look' at the forty fine mares, eight stallions and their foals. Their objective achieved, and before their welcome should pale, they departed northwards with Persian pilgrims returning from Mecca to Meshed and then alone to Baghdad. From Baghdad, having received an invitation to visit Lord Lytton the Viceroy of India, they travelled the dangerous route overland to the Persian Gulf, overcoming brigands and sickness, before sailing to Karachi, only returning to Britain in July 1879. A single mare was bought on their second expedition, in Baghdad, but, failing the Blunt's rigorous criteria of quality, it was not kept beyond a few years.

Following these two initial expeditions, the Blunts travelled in Egypt in the winter of 1880, where they first saw the stud of Ali Sharif Pasha, Lady Anne recording the horses, anecdotes and pedigrees in great detail in her journal. A visit to Arabia had to be curtailed when Wilfrid fell ill at Jeddah, and following his recovery they made for Sinai and Syria, buying some more horses from the Anazeh tribes. Although already noting that there were far fewer good mares than they had seen before, one of their purchases was the mare Rodania, from which Wilfrid later said that, 'nearly everything of the best at Crabbet' was descended.

They returned to Crabbet in May 1881 and in February the following year they purchased the small walled garden of some thirty-seven acres with the tomb of Sheykh

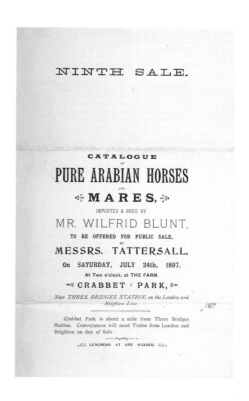

Fig. 34
Catalogue for the sale of pure Arabians at the Crabbet Stud in 1897. These were held every two years, with most of the sales going abroad. Wilfred's finances were often precarious, but Lady Anne susidised Crabbet's running costs and so the sales were not important for the money they raised. They were instead great social occasions which received considerable publicity, raising the profile of both the stud and the Arabian breed.
British Library

Obeyd on the edge of the desert nine miles north-east of Cairo, plus an extra fifteen acres outside the walls and a steam engine for irrigation for £1500. Here they planned to create a small Arabian stud in the Middle East itself but, typically, Wilfrid's outspoken support for the perceived outsider and for his own interpretation of anti-imperialism led him to agitate for the Egyptian nationalist cause. For this he was banned from Egypt for four years. After this, however, Sheykh Obeyd became their second home where they stayed most winters, receiving guests in Arab dress. Wilfrid and Lady Anne's last desert expedition together was launched from there in 1896, when they travelled between the Nile and Suez.

In Britain, Arabians were only valued for what they could contribute to other breeds and their own unique qualities were little appreciated. Even Captain Nolan, now known, if at all, as the doomed courier of the infamous confused order prompting the charge of the Light Brigade in the Crimea in 1854, but who was also the author of clear-sighted and influential works on horsemanship, thought Arabians of lesser practical use. So, though the Blunts' Arabian imports were widely noted, even appearing in *The General Stud Book* of 1881, the comment was only that 'A recent importation of Arabians from the believed Desert strains will, it is hoped, when the increase of size has been gained by training, feeding and acclimatization, give a valuable new line of blood from the original source of the English thorough-bred'.

The Blunts' work at Crabbet was of worldwide importance in maintaining the integrity of the Arabian breed. As Wilfrid emphasized, Crabbet's outstanding feature was that all of its original stock was of known pedigree and the majority of purebred Arabians today trace their lineage to the Crabbet stud. The Blunts would not buy any horses, no matter how fine, unless they could determine their exact breeding.

In this they followed in the footsteps of Muhammed Ali (1769–1849), Viceroy of Egypt, who had built up the Arabian stud later inherited by his successor Abbas Pasha I (1812–1854), the viceroy from 1848 to 1854. Abbas Pasha had sought the finest Arabian horses he could find, partly through the help of Faisal ibn Saud, and formed the most renowned Arabian stud of the time. According to the Blunts, writing in 1897, 'he ransacked the desert of Arabia and broke down, by the enormous prices he offered, the traditional refusal of the Bedouin breeders to part with their best mares'. Even a generation later, Lady Anne could still find Bedouin who well remembered these impositions: 'Salah ibn Rashid, a Bedouin Shammar spoke to me in Jan 1879 of how [he] made 3 journeys to Cairo with mares for Abbas.' The stud was partly dispersed following Abbas Pasha's assassination in 1854, but Ali Pasha Sherif, the son of the governor of Syria, acquired many of the horses and the stud still survived in the 1880s from which the Blunts eventually managed to obtain some of their most significant stock. The desert-bred horses originally acquired by the Blunts were eventually crossed with the stock purchased from Ali Pasha Sherif, the first of which came to Crabbet in 1891: the stallions Mesaoud and Merzuk and mares Sobha, Safra and Khatila. Additional stock was purchased in 1897, 1898 and 1904 (another three stallions and eight mares, with the descendants of the stallion Shahwan kept for breeding), with Ali Pasha Sherif mares kept both at Crabbet and at Sheykh Obeyd.

Wilfrid's tempestuous character and his constant, destructive affairs and indiscretions led finally to the Blunts' separation in 1906, with Lady Anne keeping Crabbet Park

and half the horses, following which she retired to Sheykh Obeyd in Cairo, where she died in 1917. Their only child, Judith Lady Wentworth, inherited the Crabbet stud after a bitter legal dispute with Wilfrid. Until her death in 1957 the stud thrived as never before – some ninety per cent of purebred Arabians today trace their lineage to Crabbet Park and it was of worldwide importance in maintaining the integrity of the breed. A charming account of life and work at Crabbet Park House and Arabian Stud during this time is given in the dictated memoirs of Fred Rice who started work there just after the First World War and rose to become head groom. It emerges that Lady Wentworth was much admired by her staff and greatly respected for her knowledge of horses (though perhaps lacking Lady Anne's scholarly depth). Upon Lady Wentworth's death in 1957, the stud passed to her manager, Cecil Covey and then to his son, who ran Crabbet until 1971, when the building of a motorway divided the property and finally forced its closure.

There is no doubt that the Blunts made a significant contribution to the history of horse breeding in Britain. They were also successful in promoting the Arabian breed and preserving its purity. At this distance in time, it is difficult to say which of the couple deserves the greater credit for these achievements. The picture is also obscured by Lady Wentworth's fierce championship of her mother at the expense of her father: 'Her devotion to this brilliant but wayward being is a record of self-sacrifice and self-effacement which will be dealt with one day ... His tyranny and spirit of discord eventually alienated him from his family, from most of his friends and from several countries.' Although she was clearly biased, however, it has to be admitted that by all accounts Wilfrid Blunt was a complex, self-centered and overbearing man, at times extremely difficult, ruthless and unpleasant. Perhaps for an evaluation of their respective contributions, we should leave the last word to Lady Anne's biographer Howard Winstone: 'In her [Lady Anne's] command of languages, her assessments of Arab notables and the oral history of the tribes, and her marshalling of facts and sources of information on horse genealogy and breeding, she was vastly his [Wilfrid's] superior and was greatly assisted by single-mindedness and the absence of preconceptions.'[3]

CHAPTER 5
THE HORSE IN MODERN BRITAIN

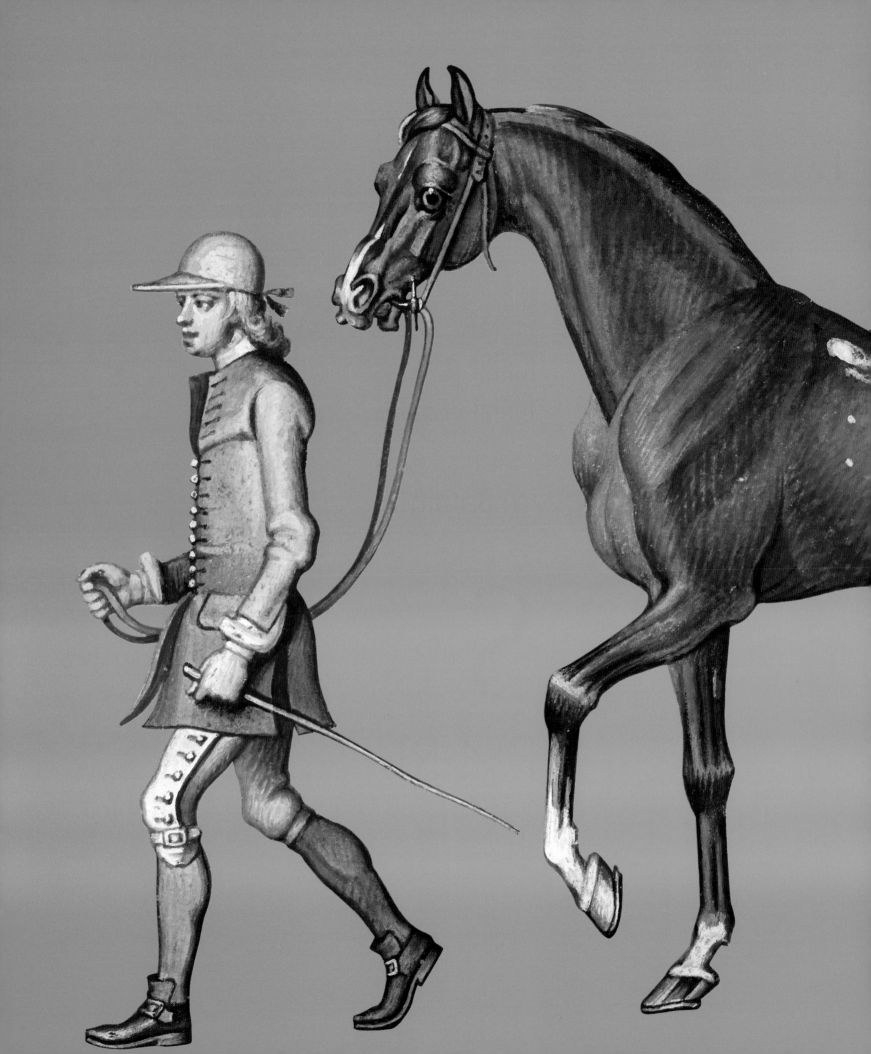

The horse in modern Britain

Fig. 36
Tina Fletcher riding Hallo Sailor as part of Great Britain's winning show jumping team in the Meydan FEI Nations Cup during the Longines Royal International Horse Show at Hickstead, England, on 30 July 2010.

Fig. 37
Painting by Sir Anthony Van Dyck dated 1633 and entitled *Charles I with M. de St Antoine*, a preparatory sketch for which is cat. 201. This fine equestrian portrait was commissioned by Charles himself and was on an unprecedented scale. The king is shown on a magnificent grey horse, with a fine head and flowing mane. Skilled horsemanship has long been regarded as the embodiment of excellence. Beside the king is Pierre Antoine Bourdin, Seigner de St Antoine, who was a master in the art of horsemanship.
The Royal Collection

S O FAR, we have reviewed the history of horses in the Middle East and in Arabia to establish the context from which the Arabian horse emerged. Our intention now is to describe the introduction of the Arabian horse into Britain from the seventeenth century onwards and the role it played in the creation of the Thoroughbred. But first, by way of background, it may be useful to consider briefly the importance of the horse in British military, social and economic history since the Norman Conquest.

The importance of horses in warfare in England was first recognized at the Battle of Hastings in 1066, when Norman knights on horseback finally broke through the wall of shields surrounding King Harold. The military significance of the mounted soldier remained undiminished until the age of mechanization and the introduction of artillery and the machine gun. Already in the reign of Edward I (1272–1307) there was a royal stud importing horses from Spain.

By the end of the medieval period changes in military technology, particularly the development of firearms, meant that the focus of breeding shifted from heavy, powerful warhorses to lighter, more nimble animals. From the reign of Henry VIII onwards there were many government instructions aimed at breeding suitable horses for warfare. As

recently been confirmed by DNA analysis. It has even been suggested (although not yet conclusively proved) that the speed gene present in the Thoroughbred may have derived from the Shetland pony. However that may be, the combination of oriental stallions with native British mares proved to be unbeatable. After the development of the breed, Thoroughbreds were exported all around the world, including to Europe and the USA. Only Thoroughbred horses are allowed to take part in Thoroughbred horse racing.

It is sometimes claimed it was James I (1603–1625) himself who had the idea of covering native mares with imported oriental stallions to produce better racehorses. This story is probably apocryphal, but oriental horses (mostly stallions) were certainly already being imported in his time. In fact, more than two hundred oriental horses (called variously Arabians, Barbs and Turks) are listed in the ancestry of the British Thoroughbred between 1614 and 1815. However, all modern Thoroughbreds trace their pedigrees back to just three stallions known as the foundation sires, two of which and possibly all three were Arabians. They are the Byerley Turk, the Darley Arabian and the Godolphin Arabian. The dark brown stallion known as the Byerley Turk (d. 1706) was named after Captain Robert Byerley. According to one tradition, the horse was captured from Ottoman troops at the Battle of Buda in Hungary in 1686 between Turkey and the Holy League. It is equally possible, however, that the horse was purchased by Captain Byerley in London after it had been imported following the relief of Vienna in 1683. However that may be, the horse was used by Byerley when he fought for William of Orange at the Battle of the

Fig. 39
Gimcrack on Newmarket Heath, with a Trainer, a Stable-Lad and a Jockey, by George Stubbs, dates from 1765 and depicts the famous racehorse Gimcrack in two scenes. On the left he is shown outside one of the rubbing-down houses at Newmarket, while on the right he is seen winning a race. The horses are shown galloping with all four of their legs outstretched, a common artistic inaccuracy before the true gait of horses was revealed through photography. This painting was sold at auction in 2011 for £22.4 million, a record for a Stubbs painting.
Private collection

Boyne in Ireland in 1690. In 1697 the Byerley Turk was retired to stud at Goldsborough Hall in North Yorkshire. Although relatively few modern Thoroughbreds trace their line back to the Byerley Turk, the famous eighteenth-century stallion Herod, also known as a founding sire, is descended from him.

The Darley Arabian (d. 1733) was a bay horse bought in Aleppo in Syria in 1702 by Thomas Darley (b. 1664), British consul to the Levant. Writing home to his brother in England, Darley described the horse as 'immediately striking owing to his handsome appearance and exceedingly elegant carriage'. He never raced, but covered mares at Aldby Park in Yorkshire between 1705 and 1719. Amongst the descendants of the Darley Arabian was the famous horse Eclipse (1766–1789), not only unbeaten in nineteen races but also a notable sire. His success on the racecourse gave rise to the phrase 'eclipse first and the rest nowhere'. He is another of the later foundation sires. Amongst the progeny of Eclipse was Pot-8-os, another very successful racehorse. It is estimated that around ninety-five percent of modern Thoroughbreds can trace their blood-lines back to the Darley Arabian, due in large part no doubt to the unrivalled success of Eclipse.

The Godolphin Arabian, a 'gold-touched bay', was imported from France in 1729 by Edward Coke (c. 1701–1733) of Longford Hall in Derbyshire. The earlier history of this horse is not clear, but according to one tradition he was originally brought from Syria to

Fig. 40
Simplified chart showing a selection of bloodlines traced back to the Darley Arabian, one of three founding sires of the Thoroughbred breed. The majority of Thoroughbreds today trace their line back to the Darley Arabian, whose descendants include the famous Eclipse.

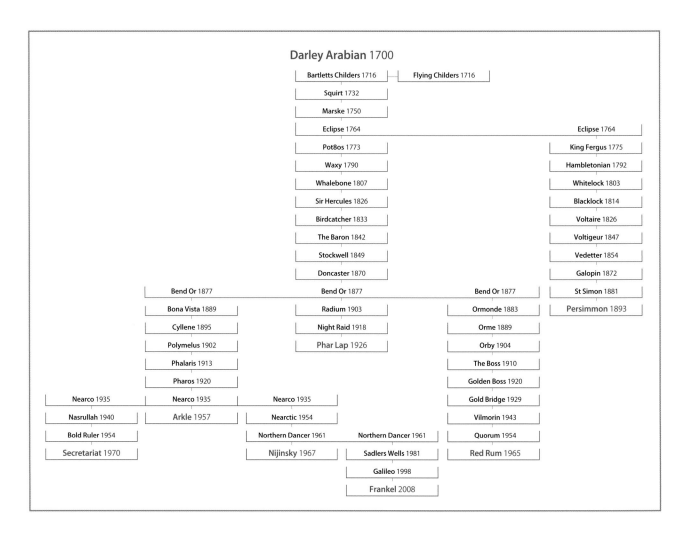

Fig. 41
Broadsheet featuring a song about Skewball. The new breed of Thoroughbred was not only widely feted in the visual arts, through portraiture, sporting print and graphic satire. Famous horses and races also featured in popular song in the eighteenth century. These broadsides, cheaply printed sheets of songs, here decorated with stock woodcuts, celebrate Skewball (sired by Godolphin Arabian in 1740) and his famous victory at the Curragh in Kildare, Ireland. The race was already a generation past by the time the sheets were printed, but the song evidently remained popular, crossing the Atlantic as 'Stewball', and survived in Britain as a folk song until the present day when taken up again in the folk revival of the 1960s.
Bodleian Library

Fig. 42
George IV when Prince of Wales (1791) by George Stubbs shows the Prince of Wales (later George IV) riding in Hyde Park, looking over the Serpentine towards Apsley House and Westminster Abbey. The prince rides a magnificent chestnut horse preceded by two dogs. He wears a blue frock coat on which is pinned the Start of the Garter, with buff breeches and a tall hat. This painting was commissioned by the Prince of Wales himself.
The Royal Collection

Tunis, where he was presented to the King of France by the Bey of Tunis. He is also known as 'the Godolphin Barb', reflecting his possible origins in or passage through Tunisia on the Barbary Coast. After the death of Edward Coke in 1733, he was taken to the stud of the 2nd Earl of Godolphin at Babraham, Cambridgeshire, where he remained until his death in 1753. He was described by the veterinary surgeon William Osmer, writing in 1756, in the following glowing terms: 'There never was a horse ... so well entitled to get racers as the Godolphin Arabian ... his shoulders were deeper, and lay farther into his back, than those of any horse yet seen. Behind the shoulders, there was but a very small space ere the muscles of his loins rose exceedingly high, broad, and expanded, which were inserted into his quarters with greater strength and power than in any horse I believe ever yet seen of his dimensions, viz fifteen hands high.'[1] It had not been intended to use the Godolphin Arabian for breeding purposes, but a union with the mare Lady Roxana, after she had rejected another stallion, led first to the famous colt Lath and then in turn Cade and Regulus. All became champion racehorses, and sired many horses. Amongst them were Matchem, a son of Cade, who is also regarded as one of the later foundation sires.

Although our purpose here is to trace the history of the horse in modern Britain, and the development there of the Thoroughbred, it should be noted that in France, too, there was much interest in the possible benefits of covering native mares with oriental stallions. This is hardly surprising as the merits of the oriental horse were known to both countries from the time of the crusades onwards. Napoleon was a great admirer of oriental horses, and himself often rode a grey Arabian named Marengo that was brought to France from Egypt as a six-year-old in 1799. He served Napoleon until the Battle of Waterloo in 1815, after which he was captured and brought to England. His skeleton is now preserved in the National Army Museum in Chelsea.

As so much importance was and still is attached to the pedigrees of Thoroughbred horses in Britain, it was necessary to record in exact detail their lineage. This was first done by James Weatherby in 1791 in The General Stud Book, which records the pedigrees of over 350 mares, all of which were descended from Herod, Eclipse or Matchem. In the United Kingdom this book is still regularly updated by the Jockey Club, and stud books are kept by appropriate regulatory bodies in other countries. The American stud book was started in 1868. Thoroughbred horses are now bred all around the world, especially in Ireland and Kentucky, USA, and Thoroughbred races are run in many parts of the world. In addition to those noted in the UK, we might mention the Kentucky Derby, the Prix de

Fig. 43
HM Queen Elizabeth II with her horse Magna Carta after it had won the Ascot Stakes on 16 June 1970. The Queen has attended the Royal Ascot races every year since 1945 and has had a number of winning horses.

l'Arc de Triomphe in Longchamp, France, and the Dubai World Cup in the United Arab Emirates. In the United Kingdom, Ireland and France, Thoroughbred horse racing takes two forms, flat racing, which we have already discussed, and national hunt racing. National hunt racing is the official name given to horse racing where the horses are required to jump over hurdles or fences. The main annual events in the UK are the Grand National at Aintree near Liverpool and the Cheltenham Gold Cup.

Although Thoroughbreds are mainly used nowadays for racing, they are also sometimes used in other equestrian sports such as show jumping, dressage and polo. Very often, however, Thoroughbreds are crossed with other breeds of horse to produce horses that are best suited for the event in question, such as jumping. This is possible because unlike racing other equestrian events are not restricted to Thoroughbreds. As a result, many of the horses competing in these events are not Thoroughbreds but many will have the blood of the Arabian horse in their veins, and it is remarkable how just one breed of horse has come to have such a major influence on the breeding of horses around the world.

Equestrian events feature in the Olympic Games, having been introduced in the second Summer Olympics in Paris in 1900, but they did not become a permanent feature until the 1912 Games in Stockholm. Nowadays, Olympic equestrian events include dressage, eventing and jumping, for each of which individual and team medals are awarded. Show jumping is also one of the five disciplines in the modern pentathlon. Outside the Olympics, in

Fig. 44
Frankel, ridden by Tom Queally, goes on to win the Queen Elizabeth II stakes at Royal Ascot racecourse on 15 October 2011. The victory led to Frankel being named as the best horse in the world in 2011, according to the World Thoroughbred Racehorse Rankings. He is owned by HRH Prince Khalid bin Abdullah of the Kingdom of Saudi Arabia.

modern Britain, horse shows (for example, the Windsor Horse Show and the London International Horse Show), horse trials or eventing (for example Badminton), dressage (training) competitions, show jumping and gymkhanas are all very popular, as they are in many parts of the world.

Horses are no longer essential in our modern age, but horse riding and sporting events involving horses are still very popular. According to the British Equestrian Trade Association there were 1.35 million horses in the UK in 2006. Foremost amongst the horse owners in the UK is HM The Queen, who owns several stud farms including the Royal Stud at Sandringham, and has bred many winners. Throughout the UK there are many clubs and societies devoted to horses, notably the Arab Horse Society based in Marlborough in Wiltshire. Their principal activity according to their website is 'to encourage the breeding and importation of pure bred Arabian horses and to encourage the introduction of Arab blood into light horse breeding.' Similar organizations are thriving in many countries in the world, all members of the World Arabian Horse Organisation, a body that gives its stamp of authority to national breeding stud books. This has ensured the purity of the Arabian breed, so that in the UK for example the Arabian horse is one of the categories in the annual Horse of the Year show. Lastly, it may be noted that the racing of purebred Arabian horses as opposed to Thoroughbreds, already popular in Saudi Arabia, the United Arab Emirates and the USA, is a fast growing activity. There are also endurance events for Arabian horses, for which they are particularly well suited.

As we have seen in this survey, the Arabian horse not only thrives today in its own right but it played a major role in the development of most types of modern horse, particularly the Thoroughbred. The climax of the British flat racing season is now Champions Day at Ascot, the racecourse near Windsor Castle founded by Queen Anne in 1711. Champions Day was first staged at Ascot on 15 October 2011 and the most prestigious race, the Queen Elizabeth II stakes, was won by Frankel, widely regarded as the greatest racehorse of modern times. From our point of view, it is of particular interest that Frankel's ancestry includes both the Darley Arabian and the Godolphin Arabian, thus taking our story full circle from the Middle East and the Arabian Peninsula to Royal Ascot.

THE CATALOGUE

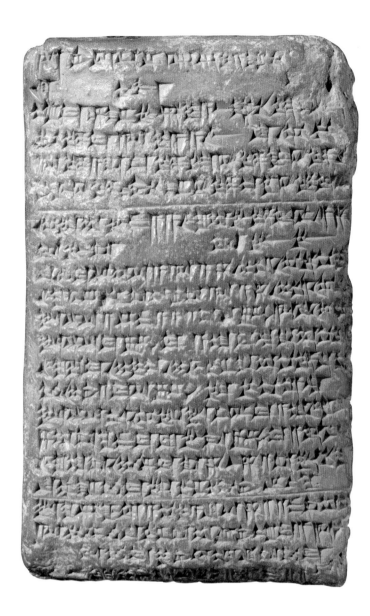

13

Letter from king Burnaburiash II to Amenhotep II

c. 1350, Middle Babylonian
el-Amarna, Egypt; acquired 1888
Clay
L 11.4 cm, W 7.3 cm
BM E29785

The Amarna letters were discovered in 1887 by a local village woman who was digging ancient mud-brick to be used as a fertilizer. This remarkable find is largely an archive of diplomatic and other correspondence sent to Amenhotep III and his son Akhenaten, with a few addressed to Tutankhamun, from subject rulers and brother kings in the Middle East. Some 380 letters survive, generally written in Babylonian Akkadian cuneiform on clay tablets. They provide invaluable details of the international relations between Egypt, Babylonia, Assyria, Mitanni, the Hittites, Syria, Canaan and even Alashiya (Cyprus).

This letter to Akhenaten from Burnaburiash II, the Kassite king of Babylonia (reigned 1359–1333 BC), concerns luxury gift exchanges, with lapis lazuli and horses sent to the Egyptian king in return for expectations of gold.

Early in his reign, relations between Burnaburiash II and Akhenaten were cordial and even included plans for a marriage alliance. As time passed, the association weakened considerably, especially when the Assyrian king Ashur-Uballit I was received in Akhenaten's court. Burnaburiash took personal offence, since he regarded the Assyrians as his vassals.

14

Letter from Tushratta of Mitanni to Amenophis III

c. 1400 BC, Mittanian
el-Amarna, Egypt; acquired 1888
Clay
L 22.2 cm, W 12.7 cm
BM E29791

The horse was introduced to Egypt in the seventeenth century BC and several tomb paintings of the New Kingdom feature gifts from Asia of horses and chariots, together with harness and equipment, helmets and coats of armour. Here, Tushratta, the king of Mitanni, sends gifts including no fewer than ten chariots with their teams of horses. Amenophis III belonged to the Egyptian 18th Dynasty.

In addition to representations in Egyptian art, chariot equipment and armour for man and horse are described in great detail in texts from the northern Mesopotamian town of Nuzi.

15

Letter from the King of Alashiya to the King of Egypt

c. 1375 BC, Middle Babylonian
el-Amarna, Egypt; acquired 1888
Clay
L 14.6 cm, W 9.8 cm
BM E29788

The possession of chariots and horses was a key indicator of power and status in the international world of the Late Bronze Age. Here, in the standard greeting format between kings of equal standing, the king of Alashiya (Cyprus) begins by reporting that his house, horses, chariots and land are well and hopes the same is true for the king of Egypt.

16

Stela, or kudurru, of Nebuchadnezzar I

c. 1100 BC, Middle Babylonian
Sippar, Mesopotamia
Limestone
H 64 cm, L 21 cm, W 18 cm
BM 90858

This very fine limestone stela, kudurru, or 'boundary stone' is sculptured in relief with symbols of deities and supernatural figures arranged in registers and columns of inscription concerning a declaration of Nebuchadnezzar I (1125–1104 BC), the king of Babylon. The figures include the goddess Gula seated upon a shrine with a dog lying beside her, and a horse's head, neck and shoulders within a double arch on a raised base or shrine.

The inscriptions record the granting of land and privileges by Nebuchadnezzar to Ritti-Marduk, the commander of his chariots, in reward for his heroic services in gaining the victory in a battle fought against Elam on the River Ulai. It describes vividly the arduous campaign, fought in the summer months, the suffering of the horses with no water in the wells, and the storm, confusion and dust of battle.

17

Cylinder seal showing a lion attacking a winged horse

1250–1200 BC, Middle Assyrian
Provenance unknown, probably Mesopotamia;
acquired 1945
Pink chalcedony
H 4.1 cm, Diam. 1.6 cm
BM 129572

This seal, probably dating to the reign of the
Assyrian king Tukulti-Ninurta I (1243–1207 BC),
shows a supernatural battle between a rearing lion
and a spirited winged horse. A wingless foal stands
between them below an uncertain device.

18

Rein-ring with goats

12th–11th century BC, Middle Elamite
Said to be from Harsin, western Iran; acquired 1931
Bronze
H 16.5 cm, W 8.4 cm, Th. 2.2 cm
BM 122700

This rein-ring is surmounted by a pair of goats with their
front feet resting on a tree. It has provision for two reins
or two sets of reins like the famous silver rein-ring from
Ur (cat. 2).

19

Horse cheekpiece in the form of a horse and rider

10th–7th century BC, Luristan
Provenance unknown, probably Luristan, Iran; acquired 1967
Bronze
H 11.8 cm, L 11.7 cm
BM 134927

The horse is a stallion and has a long tail reaching to the ground. He wears a headstall with brow-band and is being controlled by reins of twisted rope. The horse stands on a base-line and there is a hole in its body for the mouthpiece and rings above the head and the rump for the straps of the headstall. The rider, who has been represented at a very small size in comparison with the horse, wears a belted tunic and a large beehive-shaped hat. A bronze cheekpiece in the Metropolitan Museum of Art in New York is probably the companion piece to this example.

20

Horse harness-rings with goat's heads

10th–7th century BC, Luristan
Provenance unknown, probably Luristan, Iran; acquired 1930
Bronze
H 8.8 cm, W 3 cm, Th. 1.9 cm
BM 122918

A double harness-ring surmounted by the foreparts of two animals, possibly goats, joined back-to-back. The goat's heads are turned to face the front. Harness-rings such as these are thought to have been fitted to the headstalls of horses. They were probably largely decorative.

21

Horse harness-ring with head of a mouflon

10th–7th century BC, Luristan
Provenance unknown, probably Luristan, Iran; acquired 1934
Bronze
H 7.1 cm, W 8.9 cm, Diam. (central aperture) 2.4 cm
BM 123542

This consists of a ring surmounted by the head of a mouflon, a type of wild sheep with very large curled horns that was indigenous to western Iran. At the bottom of the ring, touching the tips of the mouflon's horns, are two stylized animals with curled tails, probably lions.

22

Horse harness-ring with head of a mouflon

10th–7th century BC, Luristan
Provenance unknown, probably Luristan, Iran; acquired 1930
Bronze
H 9.4 cm, W 8.4 cm, Th. 0.5 cm
BM 122917

A bronze harness-ring similar to cat. 21.

23
Horse cheekpiece in the form of a horse

10th–7th century BC, Luristan
Provenance unknown, probably Luristan, Iran; acquired 1924
Bronze
H 10 cm, L 13.9 cm
BM 135972

This horse stands on a base-line. It has a long, narrow nose and a long
tail and wears a bridle and a collar around its neck. There is a hole in
its body for the mouthpiece and two rings on the back for the straps
of the headstall.

    A bronze cheekpiece in the form of a running horse has been
found at Nimrud and cheekpieces in the form of running horses can
be seen on Assyrian reliefs dating from the reigns of Sennacherib and
Ashurbanipal. Examples, possibly of Assyrian origin, are also known
from the island of Samos. The Assyrian examples are not exactly the
same as the Luristan examples, lacking a base-line and represented
at the gallop, but it seems likely that the Assyrian cheekpieces were
inspired by those of Luristan. It is even possible that Sennacherib saw
these cheekpieces during his campaign in Luristan in 702 BC and that
they were copied on his return to Assyria.

24
Cheekpiece in the form of a goat

10th–7th century BC, Luristan
Provenance unknown, probably Luristan, Iran;
acquired 1924
Bronze
H 9.6 cm, L 10.5 cm, Th. 3.2 cm
BM 123273

The goat has curved horns and stands on a base-line, the end of which is broken away. There is a hole in its body for the mouthpiece and rings behind the neck and above the rump for the straps of the headstall. There are spikes on the inside of the cheekpiece that would have bitten into the horse's face when pressure was applied.

25
Horse bit with cheekpieces in the form of hybrid animals

10th–7th century BC, Luristan
Provenance unknown, probably Luristan, Iran; acquired 1946
Bronze
Cheekpiece I: H 9.7 cm, L 8.5 cm; cheekpiece 2: H 9.6 cm,
L 9.2 cm; W 18.1 cm
BM 134746

The bit itself is formed from a single bar with loops at either end. The cheekpieces are in the form of winged animals with human heads wearing horned headdresses. These human figures have locks of hair on either side of the head, and wear torcs or chokers. The animals have the hooves of horses or bulls, and long tails that are held high. There are two rings on the inside of each cheekpiece for the straps of the headstall, and single spikes that may have helped to control the horse.

26
Horse bit with cheekpieces in the form of hybrid animals

10th–7th century BC, Luristan
Provenance unknown, probably Luristan, Iran;
acquired 1945
Bronze
H 18.5 cm, L 16 cm (cheekpieces), W 12.5 cm
BM 130677

The bit itself is formed from a single bar with loops at either end. The cheekpieces are in the form of winged animals with human heads wearing horned headdresses.

31

Assyrian wall relief showing a lion hunt

c. 875–860 BC, Assyrian

Nimrud, North-West Palace, West Wing, from excavations of A.H. Layard, 1845–51

Gypsum

H 98 cm, W 139.5 cm, Th. 23 cm

BM 124579

This panel shows two men in a light chariot hunting lions. The figure drawing the bow is wearing a diadem (headband) knotted at the back of his head with the two ends hanging down. This is probably King Ashurnasirpal II (883–859 BC) although the king is usually shown wearing a tiara with a flat top. A wounded lion, pierced by two arrows, lies beneath the hooves of the horses. Lions were still to be found in Mesopotamia until the nineteenth century AD, usually living in reed thickets by the side of rivers. The chariot is pulled by three horses who are controlled by the driver; he holds three pairs of reins and a whip in his hands. The horses wear headstalls decorated with small bosses and they are fitted with spade-shaped blinkers. The horses have bits with large cheekpieces in a 'bow-tie' shape. Known examples of this type are sometimes barbed. This relief is carved from a type of gypsum known as Mosul marble.

32

Assyrian wall relief showing a bull hunt

c. 875–860 BC, Assyrian
Nimrud, North-West Palace, Room B, from excavations of A.H. Layard, 1845–51
Gypsum
H 93 cm, W 225 cm, Th. 9 cm (extant)
BM 124532

This panel shows the Assyrian king Ashurnasirpal II riding in a chariot while hunting bulls. One bull lies dead or dying, riddled with arrows, beneath the hooves of the chariot horses, while another bull charges the chariot from behind. The king turns, and while holding it by the horn thrusts a dagger into its neck. The chariot is being pulled by three horses wearing elaborate harness and it is being driven by a charioteer who holds three sets of reins and a whip in his hands. Behind the chariot is a horse and rider leading another horse with a richly decorated saddle-cloth with tassels, which may be a mount for the king.

33
Fragment of Assyrian wall relief

c. 875–860 BC, Assyrian
Nimrud, North-West Palace, W1; acquired 1856
Gypsum
H 55 cm, W 72 cm
BM 135741

This fragment shows the heads and chests of three chariot horses very similar to those shown on cat. 34. The whip of the charioteer is visible on the left side of the fragment. Changes in chariot design led to larger crews and teams of three and four horses. At this time only two were under the yoke; the others were 'outriggers'.

34
Assyrian wall relief showing the king riding in a chariot

c. 875–860 BC, Assyrian
Nimrud, North-West Palace, West Wing; acquired 1856
Gypsum
H 101 cm, W 86 cm, Th. 20 cm
BM 124557

This panel shows King Ashurnasirpal II, a driver and an attendant riding in a chariot. The eight reins probably indicate that there are four horses, although only three heads are shown. The king himself wears a flat-topped tiara with a small spike in the middle, and stands in the near side of the chariot. He holds in his hands a bow and a pair of arrows. The charioteer holds the reins and a whip, and the third man holds a parasol over the king's head. The three visible chariot horses wear crests surmounted by horse hair and are decorated with trappings that include tassels on their chests and on their flanks. A soldier at the front guides the team of horses over what is evidently rocky terrain, indicated by the scale pattern at the bottom of the relief. There is also a river or stream in the vicinity, indicated by wavy lines with spirals. This scene is probably part of a military campaign, with the king passing by a mountain stream.

THE CATALOGUE

35

Fragment of Assyrian wall relief showing horses and a lion

c. 875–860 BC, Assyrian
Nimrud, North-West Palace, Room WI; acquired 1856
Gypsum
H 77.8 cm, W 20.7 cm
BM 135742

Shown on this fragment are the heads and necks of two horses, apparently being controlled by a bearded man. At this time it was standard practice for a single rider to control two horses, as if he was a charioteer, leaving any fellow rider free to use his bow or spear. In this case, the second horse might be for the king, as seen in the relief, cat. 34. In front of the horses are the head and claws of a rampant lion, so the scene being shown is evidently a lion hunt, which was a royal preserve. The horses wear harness that is typical of the ninth century BC.

36

Painted sherd

9th–8th century BC, Assyrian
Provenance unknown
Pottery
H 13 cm, W 11.5 cm
BM 122083

Part of a large pottery vessel with decoration in dark brown paint showing an archer on horseback pursuing another mounted rider who is largely missing. The rider has a beard and helmet in the Assyrian style. In accordance with standard Assyrian practice, a second horse can be observed which is presumably been ridden by the man who controls the archer's horse. The horse wears a crescentic breast ornament from which are suspended bells or tassels. Assyrian texts begin to list cavalry as well as chariotry in the reign of Tukulti-Ninurta II, and they are shown widely in the art of his son Ashurnasirpal II and grandson Shalmaneser III.

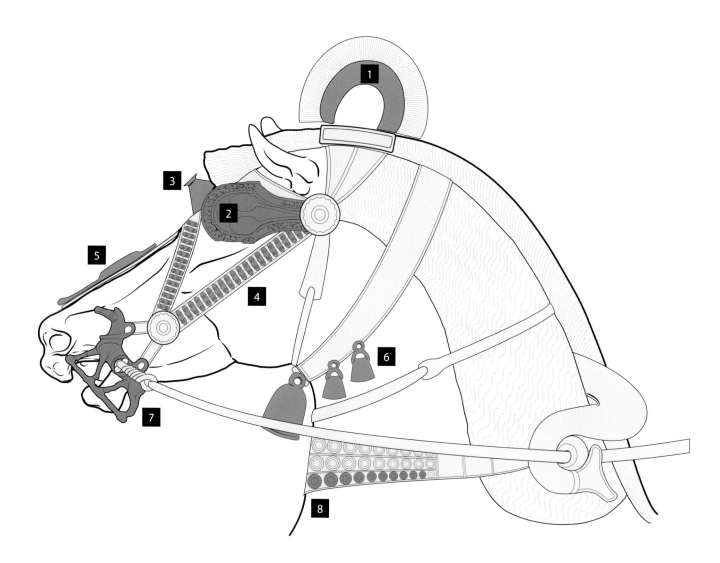

37

This diagram shows a simplified arrangement of bridle and yoke harness elements for an Assyrian chariot horse keyed to actual examples. This particular form of harness dates to the seventh century BC, though some of the actual pieces used here are earlier in date.

1   Crest holder (cat. 59).
2   Blinker (cat. 48). Blinkers are used so a harness horse can see ahead but not to the side or behind, to avoid sight of the vehicle and to prevent bickering. They are often reduced in size or omitted completely in Assyrian art, perhaps for supernatural reasons to avoid hiding the horse's eye.
3   Frontlet boss (cat. 57).
4   Bridle studs (cat. 70).
5   Frontlet (cat. 59).
6   Bells suspended from a nape strap (cat. 60–66).
7   Cheekpiece in the form of a horse (cat. 23). The cheekpieces held the mouthpiece of the bit in place and sometimes have spikes to exert extra control. This example is from Luristan, but very similar horse-shaped cheekpieces are shown used by some Assyrian horses.
8   Harness studs on the neck strap (cat. 68). The neck strap held the yoke in place.

38
Fragment of Assyrian wall relief showing a horse's head

721–705 BC, Assyrian
Khorsabad, Mesopotamia, Palace of Sargon II; acquired 1847
Gypsum
H 45.7 cm, W 33 cm
BM 118831

This fragment shows the head of a horse, probably part of a chariot scene. On the top of the horse's head is an elaborate crest, furnished with horse hair or wool, and the headstall is decorated with *phalerae* (embossed metal discs). The horse wears a brow cushion, and suspended around its neck is a series of large tassels. Around the chest of the horse is a wide band decorated with toggle-shaped (?) ornaments (see cat. 70). Scientific examination has revealed traces of red and blue paint on this relief, although they are difficult to see with the naked eye. Originally, all Assyrian reliefs were brightly coloured.

39
Fragment of Assyrian wall relief showing a horse's head

721–705 BC, Assyrian
Khorsabad, Palace of Sargon II; acquired 1847
Gypsum
H 49 cm, W 38 cm, Th. 10 cm (mounted)
BM 118833

This fragment shows the head of a horse being led by a groom, whose hand is visible holding the reins. The horse wears a curved, tapering cheekpiece that probably represents a reproduction in metal of a bone or antler cheekpiece, a padded brow cushion and a crescentic crest on top of its head. The headstall is decorated with rosettes, and tassels or corrugated metal caps (see cat. 67) hanging from the end of the brow cushion. This relief dates from the reign of Sargon II (721–705 BC).

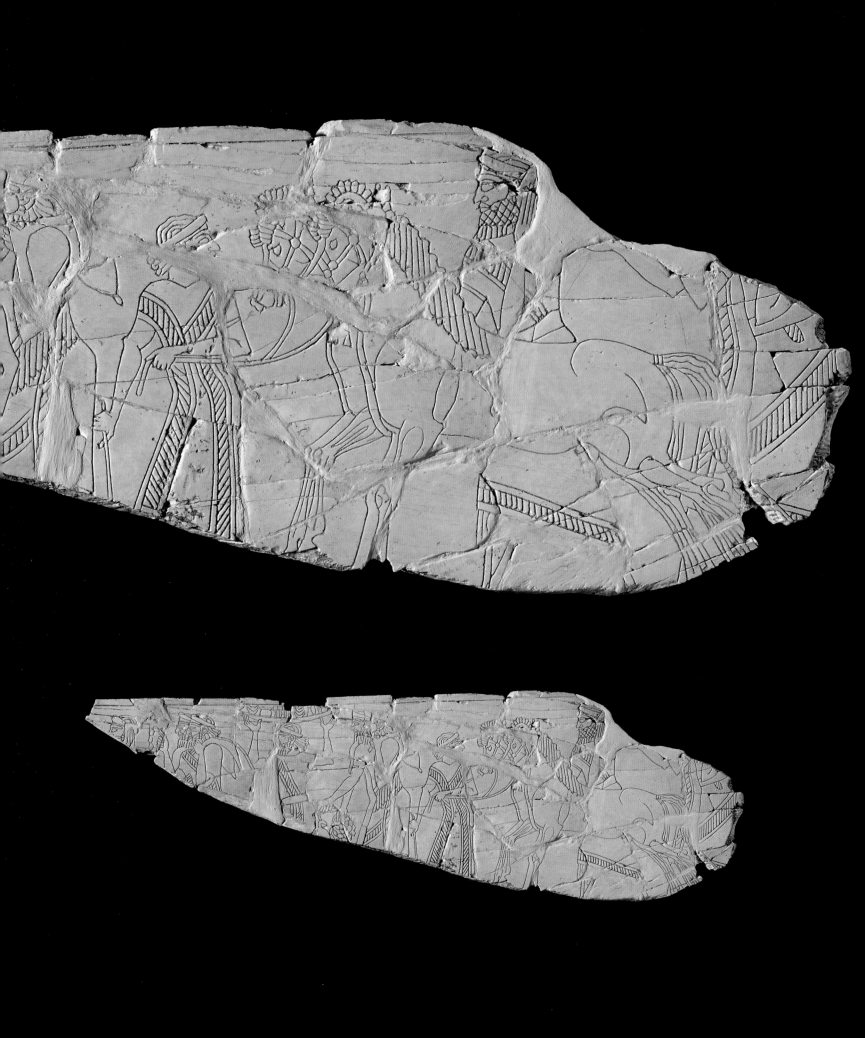

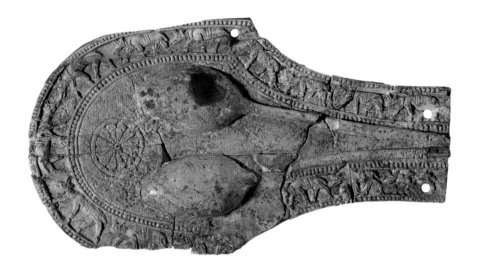

Horse's blinker ornament

9th–8th century BC, Syrian or Phoenician
Nimrud, Fort Shalmaneser, Room SW 37, excavations of BSAI,
1949–63 (ND 10752)
Ivory
L 16.1 cm, max. W 8.7 cm
BM 134960

Spade-shaped blinker ornament in carved ivory showing
in the middle two lotus buds with long stems in high relief
and an incised rosette, and around the edge of the plaque
two friezes of animals, probably goats, set between two
bands of dotted decoration. The plaque was fixed to a
backing by means of four holes around the edge.

49

Horse's blinker ornament

9th–8th century BC, Syrian or Phoenician
Nimrud, Fort Shalmaneser, Room SW 37, excavations of British
School of Archaeology in Iraq 1949–63 (ND 10802)
Ivory
L 8.2 cm, W 6.1 cm
BM 2011,6001.745

Shield-shaped blinker ornament in carved ivory with
decoration that includes an Egyptian *wedjat*-eye (eye
of Horus) and a human arm and hand with bangles on
the upper arm. There are holes along the base of the
plaque for attachment.

50

Blinker ornament

9th–8th century BC, Syrian or Phoenician
Possibly from Nimrud
L 16.8 cm, max. W 8 cm
BM 91337

Spade-shaped blinker ornament in bronze with embossed
decoration showing three lotus buds on long stems in
the centre. Two embossed ribs repeat the outline of
the plaque at the front, and there are four holes for
attachment.

51

Horse's blinker ornament

9th–8th century BC, Syrian or Phoenician
Nimrud, Fort Shalmaneser, Room SW 37, excavations of BSAI, 1949–63
(ND 10495)
Ivory
L 12.8 cm, W 7.6 cm
BM 2011,6001.637

Spade-shaped blinker ornament in carved ivory showing
a sphinx with a woman's head and lion's body wearing a large
collar. There is a border of guilloche ornament around the
outside of the plaque, and there are four large holes for
securing it to a backing. The Egyptian style of the sphinx shows
that this plaque was made in Phoenicia (Lebanon) or Syria.

52

Horse's blinker ornament

9th–8th century BC, Syrian or Phoenician
Nimrud, Fort Shalmaneser, Room T 10, excavations
of BSAI, 1949–63 (ND 11200)
Gypsum
L 11.3 cm, W 7.9 cm
BM 132997

Spade-shaped blinker ornament with a large
bud in high relief in the centre. Two faint lines
below the bud are probably meant to indicate
the stem. There is a sunken border around
the edges of the plaque in which are holes for
attachment.

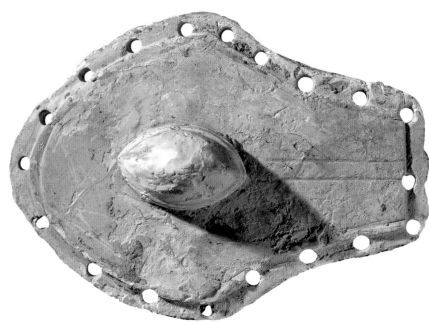

53

Horse's blinker ornament

9th–8th century BC, Syrian or Phoenician
Nimrud, Fort Shalmaneser, Room SW 37, excavations of BSAI,
1949–63 (ND 9449)
Ivory
L 6.8 cm, W 7.1 cm
BM 2011,001.472

Plain shield-shaped blinker ornament with large holes
for attachment along the base and for a short distance
along one side.

54
Horse's frontlet ornament

9th–8th century BC, Syrian or Phoenician
Nimrud, Fort Shalmaneser, Room SW 37, excavations
of BSAI, 1949–63 (ND 10511)
Ivory
H 10 cm, W 5.6 cm
BM 2011,6001.643

Triangular-shaped horse's frontlet or face-
piece ornament in carved ivory decorated with
two naked women standing on a lotus flower.
They wear bangles on their wrists and ankles.
There is a row of large holes at the top of the
plaque for attachment.

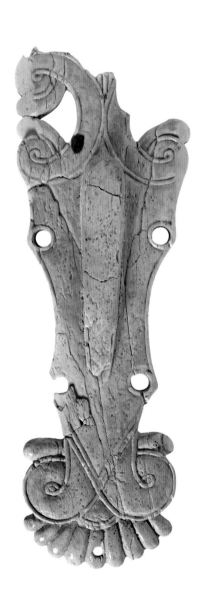

THE CATALOGUE

55
Horse's frontlet ornament

9th–8th century BC, Syrian or Phoenician
Nimrud, Fort Shalmaneser, Room SW 37, excavations
of BSAI, 1949–63 (ND 10515)
Ivory
H 15.0 cm, W 5.3 cm
BM 2011,6001.644

Horses frontlet or face-piece ornament in carved
ivory with double volute ornaments at the top
and a palmette combined with a lotus flower at
the bottom. There are four holes for attaching
this ornament to a backing.

56
Horse's frontlet ornament

9th–8th century BC, Syrian or Phoenician
Nimrud, Fort Shalmaneser, Room T 10, excavations of BSAI,
1949–63 (ND 12503)
White stone
H 11.1 cm, W 7.9 cm
BM 140417

Horse's frontlet or face-piece ornament in white
stone of quadrilateral shape tapering towards the
bottom. There is a sunken border around the edges
of the plaque in which are holes for attachment.

57

Horse harness boss

8th–7th century BC, Assyrian
Nimrud, Iraq, excavations of A.H. Layard, 1845–51
Bronze
H 3.5 cm, W 6.3 cm
BM N.116

Hollow bronze boss with flared sides, a flat top
and a ring fastener inside for attachment. Such
bosses can be seen on Assyrian reliefs mounted
on the horse's forehead above the frontlet.
Alternatively, elaborate bosses are sometimes
mounted on the headstall.

58

Horse's frontlet ornament

9th–8th century BC, Phoenician or Syrian
Nimrud, Fort Shalmaneser, Room SW 37, excavations
of BSAI, 1949–63 (ND 10435)
Ivory
H 10.2 cm, W 5.9 cm
BM 2011, 6001.620

Horses frontlet or face-piece ornament in carved
ivory. The decoration includes a *wedjat*-eye (eye
of Horus), a human arm and hand and a lotus
flower. There is a row of large holes at the top of
the plaque for attachment.

59

Bronze replica of horse harness crest

This is a copy of a bronze object found in the Assyrian destruction level
at Lachish dating from 701 BC, when Sennacherib attacked the city. The
original is now in the Rockefeller Museum in Jerusalem. It has been variously
interpreted as a helmet crest or a horse harness crest. The object is crescent-
shaped and hollow, and would have held an upstanding crest made from
textile or horse hair. Such crests can be seen on Assyrian reliefs worn on the
top of horse's heads.

60–66
Horse harness bells

9th–7th century BC, Assyrian
Nimrud, North-West Palace, Room AB, excavations of A.H. Layard, 1845–51
Bronze
H from 4.85 cm to 8.2 cm
BM N.157, N.182, N.177, N.155, N.199, N.193, N.215

In two cauldrons in the 'Room of the Bronzes' (AB) in the North-West Palace at Nimrud, Layard found what he rightly identified as 'ornaments of horse and chariot furniture'. Amongst them was a large collection of nearly eighty bells which are now in the British Museum. They include large examples with rounded shoulders, a ring at the top and a flange at the bottom, smaller straight-sided examples with loop holders at the top, and bells with straight flaring sides and a figure-of-eight holder at the top. A noticeable feature of all these bells is that they have clappers in the form of thick iron rods. These clappers sometimes survive intact, but are mostly missing.

The Assyrian reliefs clearly show that bells were suspended around horses' necks. From the time of Tiglath-pileser III (744–727 BC) onwards, bells or tassels sometimes hang from a band or strap, sometimes of plaited leather and usually referred to as a nape strap. Both draught and cavalry horses are shown wearing bells, the purpose of which seems to have been both decorative and to intimidate the enemy with their noise. Large numbers have been found in Urartu, the Caucasus and western Iran, suggesting that the fashion for using them as horse trappings comes from those areas. It is interesting that these are the same regions, to the north and north-east of Assyria, which also bred horses.

67

Tassel-holder, part of horse harness

8th–7th century BC
Nimrud, North-West Palace, Room AB, excavations of A.H. Layard, 1845–51
Bronze
Max. L 10.16 cm, max. diam. 4.5 cm
BM N 281, N 282, N 546

Bronze caps with corrugated sides and a hole in the top, for fixing to a metal rod. The rods have a loop at the top for attachment and a stop at the bottom to keep the cap in position. Sometimes three of these caps are suspended from a small holdfast. They are either harness ornaments in their own right or they are meant to be tassel-holders.

68

Harness studs

9th–7th century BC
Nimrud, excavations of BSAI, 1949–1963
Bronze
Diam. 1.1 cm
BM 1984,0205.266

Small bronze bosses used for decorating a horse's harness. These are hammered from sheet-metal and inserted into leather harness straps.

69

Toggle

9th–7th century BC
Nimrud, Fort Shalmaneser, Room SE 11, excavations of BSAI, 1949–63 (ND 7814)
White stone
H 12 cm, max. diam. 4.5 cm
BM 140336

Oval stone toggle with a groove around the centre. Toggles are shown in various contexts on Assyrian reliefs, but in connection with horses they are used to fix securely the trappers or horse-blankets sometimes worn by cavalry and draught horses. This is particularly clear on reliefs of Ashurbanipal (668–631 BC).

70

Harness ornaments

9th–7th century BC
Nimrud, North-West Palace, Room AB,
excavations of A.H. Layard, 1845–51
White stone
L 2.4 cm, W 0.9 cm, Diam. 1.2 cm
BM N 2081

Elongated oval studs with rib decoration
and a projection underneath with two holes,
for fixing to a background. Such ornaments
are to be seen on breast straps and other
elements of harness.

71

Harness studs

9th–7th century BC
Nimrud, North-West Palace, Room AB, excavations
of A.H. Layard, 1845–51
Shell
Diam. c. 1–1.5 cm
BM 140345, 1994,1105.129

These studs have a flanged base and a domed top.
They would have been used to decorate leather straps
and items of harness.

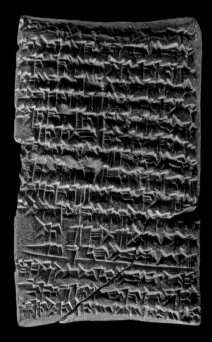

72

Cuneiform tablet

7th century BC, Assyrian
Nineveh, Mesopotamia; acquired 1882
Baked clay
L 16.2 cm, W 8.6 cm
BM 1882,0323.1

This tablet contains an inscription describing an elaborate ritual to avert headache, plague and pestilence affecting the royal horses or soldiers.

73

Cuneiform tablet

7th century BC, Assyrian
Nineveh, Ashurbanipal's Library
Baked clay
L 5.7 cm, W 5.7 cm
BM K.8197

This tablet describes the fable of the ox and the horse and details a dispute over their relative merits. Here, the horse expounds on itself. The tablet is part of a library of cuneiform tablets believed to have been collected by or for King Ashurbanipal (c. 668–631 BC).

74

Cuneiform tablet

7th century BC, Assyrian
Nineveh, Ashurbanipal's Library
Baked clay
H 7.7 cm, W 4.8 cm
BM K.6163

Part of a clay tablet, containing the question to the gods about the suitability of a particular horse to pull the chariot of Marduk, the patron god of Babylon. It includes a short hymn to the horse and an incantation to be spoken into its right ear.

84

Fragment of stone relief showing a charioteer

6th–5th century BC, Achaemenid
Persepolis, Iran, from the top register of the east wing of the northern staircase
of the Apadana; acquired 1817
Limestone
H 56 cm, W 88 cm
BM 118843

The figure is standing in a chariot box, the front part of which is preserved.
It has rosettes around the edge. There is a quiver on the front of the box
and another (only the top of which is visible) is mounted on the side. The
charioteer holds a stick and reins that pass over the backs of two horses and
run through a terret or rein-ring that is set on the yoke. There is a

fan-shaped yoke ornament above the terret and a tassel hangs down from
the yoke.

The heads of the horses are preserved on a fragment that is now in
the Miho Museum in Japan. This fragment was found with the main piece
at Persepolis in 1811 but was apparently given to Sir Gore Ouseley and
became part of his collection. It passed to his son Sir Frederick Ouseley
who founded a school called St Michael's College in Tenbury, England.
After the school closed down in 1985 the relief was sold at auction and was
eventually purchased by the Miho Museum. A cast of this piece is shown
in the exhibition. Originally this relief would have been part of a scene
that showed a procession of Persian guards followed by an usher and four
grooms carrying whips, saddle-cloths and a stool, then an usher with three
horses and grooms, and finally another usher with two royal chariots.

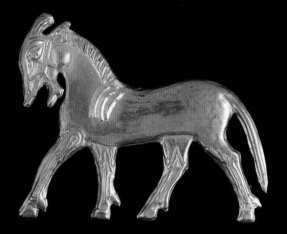

101
Gold sheet cut-out figure of horse

5th–4th century BC, Achaemenid
Oxus Treasure; A.W. Franks bequest 1897
Gold
H 2.8 cm, L 3.6 cm
BM 123945

Gold sheet cut-out figure of a horse, embossed with muscles indicated by punching, forelock swept back and mane pulled but long at the neck in typical Achaemenid style.

102
Gold sheet cut-out figure of a horse

5th–4th century BC, Achaemenid
Oxus Treasure; A.W. Franks bequest 1897
Gold
H 4.2 cm, L 5.5 cm
BM 123947

The horse, possibly intended to be a Nesaean, is more finely finished than the above, with punched and incised details of harness, mane (though not dressed in typical Persian style) and tail. The mouth is pierced, probably for wire reins now missing. The forelock is shown tied into a splayed tuft on the poll and there is a loop on the horse's back, probably for a wire yoke. If so, then this is a draught horse for another chariot model.

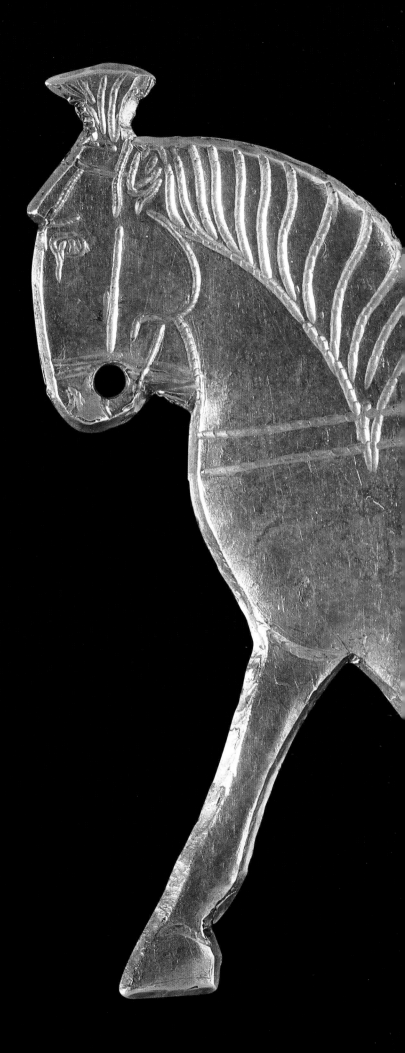

103

Horse harness ornament or shield-boss

5th–4th century BC, Achaemenid
Oxus Treasure; A.W. Franks bequest 1897
Silver, gold
Diam. 9.7 cm
BM 123925

This ornament contains a hunting scene involving three riders on horseback. It consists of a circular disc with gold overlay and an embossed centre pierced by five holes. There is a guilloche pattern around the edge. The hunters are wearing Median dress with caps and ornate trouser-suits. They ride without stirrups, which were not known at this time. The horses wear patterned saddle-cloths secured with a breast strap and fringed at the back, and their tails are tied in mud-knots with bows. Two of the horsemen converge on a pair of ibexes, one of which has already been struck by a spear. One of these horsemen is armed with a spear and the other with a bow and arrow. The third horseman, again armed with a spear, pursues two deer, one of which has a broken spear sticking into it. In front of the ibexes is a hare. The figure-of-eight or waisted shield types at Persepolis are sometimes represented with similar circular fittings in the centre, but the similarities are not close, so it is more likely that this piece is a harness ornament, or *phalera*.

114

Athenian red-figured *hydria* (water-jug) with two Greeks fighting a mounted Persian

c. 360–330 BC
From Cyrenaica (Libya); acquired 1866
Ceramic
H 29.5 cm
BM 1866,0415.244

On the right a bearded Persian is mounted on a rearing white horse and aims a spear or javelin at a Greek warrior on foot. The Persian wears a soft skin hat (*kidaris*) with its long ear-flaps hanging down, an oriental trouser-suit, and soft shoes. The young warrior is equipped with a white *pilos*-style helmet, circular shield and a *chlamys* round his back. He thrusts up with his long spear at the Persian. On the left a wavy-haired archer, wearing a short chiton and with a quiver at his hip, aims his bow at the Persian while sheltering behind his companion's shield.

This is one of the latest red-figured Athenian vases to show a fight between Greeks and Persians.

115

Plaque showing a mounted cataphract

3rd–2nd century BC, Late Hellenistic or Early Parthian
Mesopotamia; acquired in 19th century
Baked clay
H 15.2 cm, W 19 cm, Th. 2.3 cm
BM 91908

A warrior seated on a rearing horse, wearing a round helmet with a rim
at the bottom and a suit of scale or lamellar armour, holds a long spear
with which he is fighting a lion. The horse wears a bridle and has a bushy
tail. The plaque is pinkish-cream in colour and has a border all around
the edge. There are two holes at the top of the plaque to hang it up or
to fix it to a background.

125

Handle in the form of a horse's head

1st–2nd century AD, Parthian, Ptolemaic or Roman
Provenance unknown; acquired 1972
Bone
L 9.8 cm, W 2.7 cm, Th. 1.3 cm
BM 135718

Length of bone, hollowed out in the middle, carved in the
form of a horse's head and neck. The horse wears a headstall
and brow-band, and has a long and flowing mane. There are
holes at either end of this handle, one of which must be to
fix it in position.

126

Stamp seal with a winged horse

4th century AD, Sasanian period
Provenance unknown; acquired 1841
L 1.9 cm, W 1.6 cm
Jasper
BM 119564

This domed stamp seal has an engraved design showing
a winged horse (Pegasus) surrounded by an inscription
in Pahlavi letters. The Pahlavi script was used to write
inscriptions in the Middle Persian language.

127

Silver gilt plate with hunting scene

5th–7th century AD, Sasanian
Provenance unknown; A.W. Franks bequest 1897
Silver with traces of surface gilding
Diam. 27.6 cm, max. H 5 cm
BM 124092

This plate shows a Sasanian king on horseback hunting lions. He holds a lion club in his left hand, and slashes at a lion with a sword held in his right hand. Blood spurts from the wound inflicted on the lion. A lioness leaping up in front of the horse has already been wounded in the same place on the back of the neck. The lion and lioness are probably the parents of the cub being held by the king. The scales at the bottom of the scene indicate the action is taking place in rocky or mountainous countryside. The king is identifiable as Bahram V (421–439) through his crenellated crown with a crescent and a globe that is also found on coin portraits of this reign. The king wears an elaborate belted tunic, probably of silk, and leggings over his trousers. A richly decorated quiver is suspended from his belt. The diadem ties (ribbons) attached to the king's crown, shoulders, shoes, and the horse's rump, are all symbols of the monarch's kingly glory (*khwarna/ farr*). The king sits on a patterned saddle cloth with his feet hanging loose, not supported in stirrups. The horse has a bridle decorated with *phalerae* and wears tasselled bands around breast and rump. The two 'balloons' attached to the back of the horse are sometimes thought to be fly-whisks. The plate has a ring foot and the decoration is engraved and chased. Although the plate depicts Bahram V, it may have been made later than his reign, possibly in Afghanistan or north-west India.

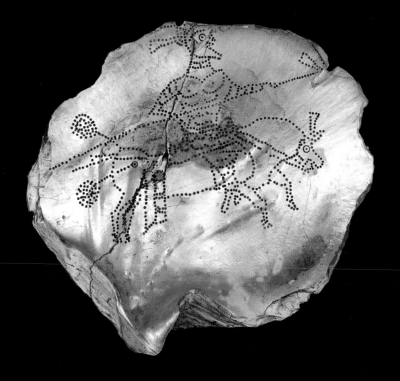

128

Oyster shell showing horse and rider

5th–7th century AD, Sasanian
Provenance unknown; acquired 1996
Shell
H 13.1 cm, W 13.7 cm, D 1.5 cm
BM 1996,1001.1

The decoration on this oyster shell has been made with incised dots. The bearded rider wears a cuirass and holds a long lance. He sits on a saddle-cloth and behind him is a quiver. The diadem ties (ribbons) on the rider's headdress, the lance and the horse's head show that the rider is a king. Floating behind the horse are two 'balloons' or fly-whisks. The diadem ties and the fly-whisks are characteristic features of Sasanian art and can be found on the silver plate, cat. 127. This shell is probably of similar date.

129

Complete Holy Quran

16th century AD
H 36 cm, W 24 cm (closed), 48 cm (open)
King Abdulaziz Public Library, 3929

A complete *mushaf* from Surah Al-Fātihah to Surah Al-Nās
written within multicoloured borders in black ink, gold
leaf and liquid turquoise. Diacritical marks were used to
vowelize the Speech of Allah. Extra attention was given to

Complete Holy Quran

19th century AD
H 35 cm, W 22 cm (closed), 40 cm (open)
King Abdulaziz Public Library, 2332

This complete *mushaf* from Surah Al-Fātihah to Surah Al-Nās is written in black ink with diacritic marks, inside golden, green, red and blue colou borders. The footnotes of the first and last pag are embellished with gold-leaf botanical design Inside the ruler margins are impressions in the shape of Islamic decorations. The blue colour v extracted from turquoise that lends a beautiful appearance to the decoration. At the beginning the *mushaf*, an index of the *surahs* (chapters) wa written in italics inside small squares by the fam Iranian calligrapher Muhammad Sharif Afshar, ir Jumādā Al-Awwal 1270 AH (AD 1853). This manuscript is deemed to be from the imperial manuscripts, which are written for a ruler with g care and precision over a long period. It is bour with impermeable Persian leather. Paper extract from rice husks was placed in between the manuscript's pages to prevent the colour from overlapping.

Complete Holy Quran

7th century AD
Saudi Arabia
H 18 cm, W 11 cm (closed), 24 cm (open)
King Abdulaziz Public Library, 1600

This complete *mushaf* from Al-Fātihah to Surah Al-Nās is written in black ink, with diacritical marks, inside red and blue ruled margins. It was written during Ramadan in 1025 AH (AD 1616), n Mecca in front of the Holy Ka'bah, and was compared to a copy written by the noble scholar Al-Mulla Ali Al-Qari who died in the year 1014 AH.

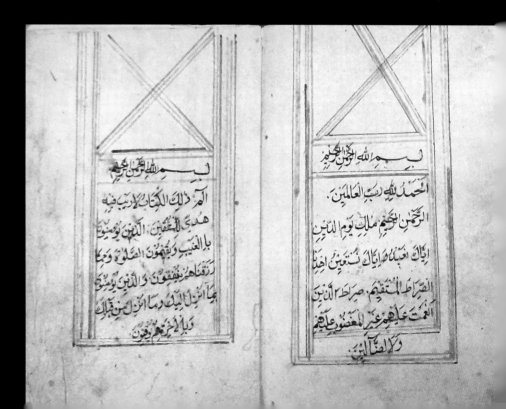

لم يجبزه قول معظم العلماء قال وهذا يجمع على قول مالك فان اخرجها مما
قد لم يكن معها غيرها لم يجبزه فرذلك واحدا فى مذهبه وانكان معما محلل
لكنه فى ذلك روايتان احدهما المنع كالم كن محلل وفى المشهورة عنه
قال ابن عبد البر قال مالك لنا هذا يقول سعيد بن المسيب وهو المحلل ولا يعيب
المحلل ولكن قال قال ابن عباس وهذه المشهورة عنه الرواية الثانية انه
يجبزه بالمحلل لقول سعيد بن المسيب قال ابو محمد والوجود من قوليه وقول
ابن المسيب وجمهور اهل العلم واختياره ابن الموازعين وفصل
وجهة هذا القول انه لا يعود المحرز بسببه محال انه متى جاء له
ازكان غاليا لم يكن جماله لان الانسان لا يبذل الجعل من ماله للغير
على عمل يعمله قال زكاك فاذ اكان سابقا فاخرز بسبق نفسه لكان
قدبذل من مال نفسه جعلا على عمل بعمله هو وهذا اخترجازه فأنه
لا يحصل له نفذ خائفة ثالوايضا فنيه سبق الثان لان امانت
بعمل واماانت سلم وهذا شان النا لا يخلفه الجعل اذكان اجنبيا
فأنه غار وله حالة ثالوا هذا على هذا يكون مع بذل المال الذي جعله
للسابق لانه بذله على عمل و نقد وجدك الرمرذلك يخلفظ ثالوا
وهذا على اصول اهل المدينة الزمر ثانه بلزمه الوفاء بالوعد اذا
قبض تطريرا كنت كان قال لغيرك تزوح مها وانا انقذعنك المهر واستدت
اكالو كل وانا وقيمنك وتعهدنا وهو بلاخلاف عندنا وانما القام
يتفض تطريرا فنبه بها على الخلاف بين الاصحاب واصحاب القول

المال بذله لئن كان اقى على طاعته الله فيا خلب اخذه كما يذكرعن الشانى
انه كان بساكل فى بعض اهله عن مسألة ويقول لئن اجاب فيط اعطيته درهما
وهذا اكقل الامام من تلك قبلك ذله سلبه وفين جاء من راس مش ذورس
المشركين خله كذ اوكذا ما يجعل فيه الجعل كن فضل غيره عن على بر ليكون
ذلك مرغبا للنفس سرما سمان به على با عن الله درمضا ن له ولهذا
استنا المبعى على عليه وسلم عن اللعو الباطل نهذ اتمير وهذا
المذهب وتخريج فصل وقالت طائفة اخر يجبز زيذ لك الجعل من
الامام واجنبى وان ما يكون الباذل احدهما جائز فشرط ا انلابو لايو السبق
الى الخر يجبل على امكان معها غيرها كان ارلمن يليه وان كان اشنين نفط
كان لمن حضر وسرهذه القول ان محرم السبق لايموذ اليه سبقه بحال
وهذا احدى الروايتين عن مالك وقال ابكر الطرطوشى وهو قول
المشهور وقال ابن عمرن عبد البر انقط بمن ريمالك والاوزاعى وان
الاشياء المسبق لارجوا المسبقط على قال يريد ان السبق لرجح
عندهؤلاء المجدورة بعل قال وخالفهم الشافعى وابواحنيته والمثوث
دغيرهم فعارهذا اللغول اذا سبق الخرج كان سبقه طعمة لمن حضر
سواء شرط ذلك اولا ويكفع مالك روايته ثانية اسواها ابن وهب
عنه انه اذالها الشترط السبق لمن سبق جاز سواءكان مخرجا اولا يكن
وعلى هذه الرواية السبق لمن يكون طعمته لمن حضر واخايكون السابق ان كانت
شط على هذه الرواية ان يكون السبق طعمة للحاضرين فذ الله الطرطوشى

132
Al-Furusiyya ah-Hemmareh

20th century AD
Saudi Arabia
Manuscript
H 21 cm, W 15 cm
King Abdulaziz Public Library, 5871

This is a modern copy of a manuscript by Mohammed ibn
Abu Bakr ibn Ayoub ibn al-Qayyim al-Joziah written before
the author's date in 751 AH/AD 1350. The copy was verified by
Sheikh Abdul Qadir Hamza who died in Mecca in 1352 AH/
AD 1972. This manuscript has a good deal of information
about *furusiyya* or horsemanship. The three original disciplines
of *furusiyya* are proper horsemanship (including veterinary
aspects of caring for horses, and riding techniques), archery,
and charging with a lance. Ibn al-Qayyim al-Joziah adds
swordsmanship as a fourth discipline in his manuscript.

135
Ewer with inlaid decoration

c. AD 1232
Mosul, Iraq
Brass inlaid with silver and copper
H 30.4 cm, W 22 cm, D 21.5 cm
BM 1866,1229.61

This splendid ewer, made of hammered sheet brass and
engraved and inlaid with silver and copper, is celebrated
as one of the finest and most important examples of
Islamic metalwork, carrying information about its maker
and place of production. This identification, inscribed
in Arabic around the neck of the ewer, states that the
object was decorated by Shuja ibn Mana al-Mawsuli
('of Mosul', in modern Iraq) in Rajab 629 AH/April AD
1232. It is also commonly known as the Blacas Ewer,
after the Duke of Blacas, a nineteenth-century French
Ambassador to the Kingdom of the Two Sicilies whose
collection was acquired by the British Museum in 1866.
Although missing its spout and foot, the ewer's body and
neck are richly decorated with a series of scenes, many
of them contained within medallions. Scenes showing
horses include a mounted warrior with a sword and shield
fighting with a soldier on foot, a horseman out hunting
with a feline creature (possibly a cheetah) seated on the
rump of his horse, and an archer on horseback shooting
at what appears to be a boar jumping up at the back of
his horse. A benedictory Arabic inscription circling the
lower body of the vessel reads: 'Glory, long life, and ease,
(God's) sympathy, blessing, health, felicity, victory over
enemies, superiority, and (God's) protection forever for
its owner.'

136

Boss depicting archers

Late 12th–early 13th century AD
Kashan, Iran
Ceramic with underglaze painted decoration
Diam. 28 cm
BM 1964,1013.2

The scene on this boss, painted in black under a transparent turquoise glaze, shows two mounted archers shooting arrows at a target mounted on a tall pole. This may be an early representation of a sport known as *qabaq* in which archers aimed at a gourd mounted on top of a pole. Such activities played an important part in developing equestrian and archery skills. The purpose of this boss is unknown.

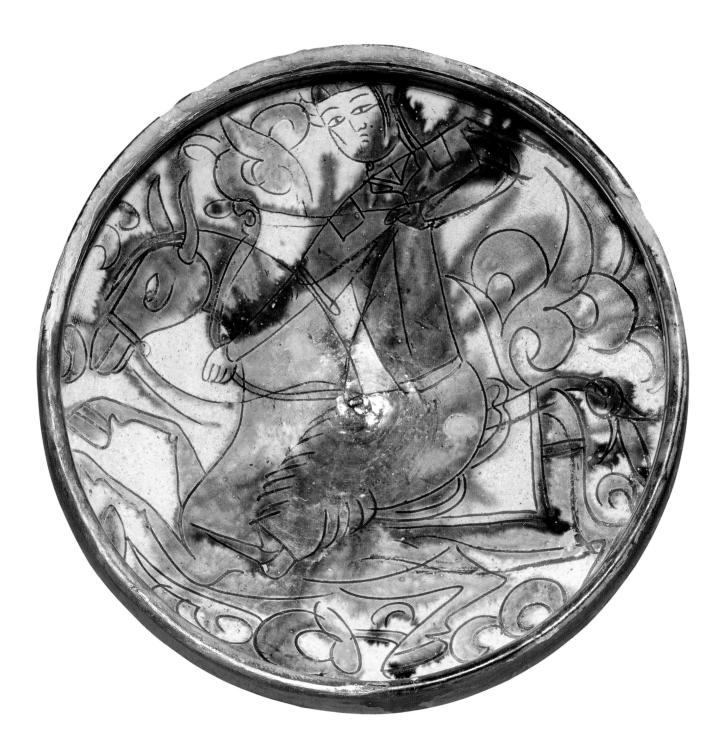

137

Sgraffiato bowl depicting a mounted archer

c. 1250
Aleppo, Syria
Ceramic with underglaze, incised and painted decoration
Diam. 26.3 cm, H 11.7 cm
BM 1931,0716.1

This bowl shows a helmeted warrior on horseback drawing a bow. He wears a belted tunic with ornamental bands on the sleeves. He sits on a saddle that is mounted on a plain saddle-cloth. The reins appear to be hanging loose, so the rider was presumably controlling the horse with his knees. The technique known as *sgraffiato* involves incising a design into a slip on the surface of the vessel before firing. After firing, the scene is then painted, in this case green, brown and purple, and covered with a clear glaze.

138

Pilgrim flask

c. 1250–75, Mamluk
Egypt or Syria; Slade bequest, 1869
Enamelled glass
H 23 cm, L 23 cm, W 16.2 cm
BM 1869,0120.3

Glassmakers active in Egypt and Syria during the thirteenth and fourteenth centuries were known for their fine work in the production of mosque lamps, bottles, beakers and flasks. Some scholars suggest that Syrian glassmakers were the first to use the technique of enamelling and gilding on glass beginning in the late twelfth century.

This object is modelled after a pilgrim flask and was skilfully painted in red, white, blue, green, yellow, mauve and greyish-black enamels, with the design executed in gold outlined in red. One side is decorated with a large

palmette filled with a scrolling foliate design. The other two sides depict a seated banqueter and seated femail lutenist, each with a mounted rider shown above. The riders, dressed in long tunics and flowing cloaks, are identified as Christian both by their clothing and their rounded broad-brimmed 'kettle' helmets associated with the Crusader infantrymen. One impales a wolf or a bear with a couched lance, the other shoots a lion (?) with a crossbow – both western weapons. Their horses, a grey and a chestnut, are wearing bridles with curb bits, decorated neck bands, breast bands and striped saddle-cloths.

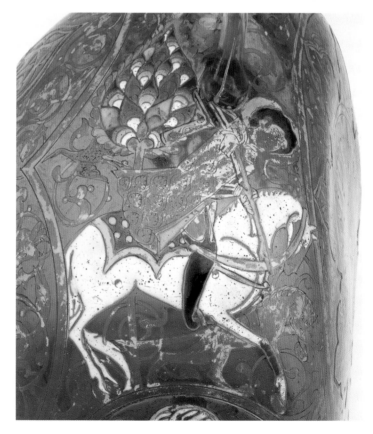

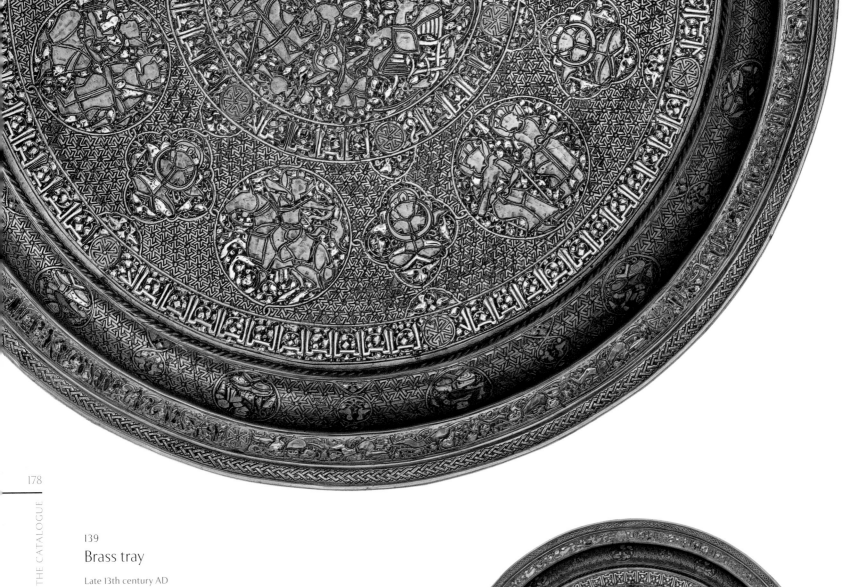

139

Brass tray

Late 13th century AD
Probably western Iran; Henderson bequest, 1878
Brass inlaid with silver and gold
Diam. 46.3 cm
BM 1878,1230.706

This brass tray is inlaid with silver and gold. In the centre is a large
medallion with a king seated on a throne, holding a cup, while two armed
attendants stand and two others shoot arrows. In front are two lions
and a double-headed eagle. Around the centre are six circular and six
quatrefoil medallions. Three of the circular medallions show figures
on horseback hunting animals. Certain stylistic elements recalling the
thirteenth-century metalwork tradition of Mosul (Iraq) suggest the
possibility that objects such as this salver, although probably produced
in Iran, were made by craftsmen relocated from Mosul to the Ilkhanid
Mongol court in Tabriz (western Iran) subsequent to the Mongol
conquest of Mosul in 1261.

140

Brass bowl

14th century AD
Fars, Iran; Burges bequest, 1881
Brass inlaid with silver and gold
H 11.8 cm, Diam. 23.7 cm
BM 1881,0802.21

This incised brass bowl with inlaid silver decoration has scenes of life at court interspersed with four medallions formed from interlacing bands inscribed with blessings and verses. Within the medallions, figures on horseback hunt wild animals. Inlaid metal wares produced in this round-bottomed shape as well as in the form of candlesticks, ewers and other portable objects, decorated with detailed miniature courtly scenes and bold inscriptions, are typical of metalwork production in the region of Fars, a province in south-western Iran, in the late fourteenth and early fifteenth centuries.

141

Candlestick holder

13th–14th century AD
Konya, Turkey; acquired 1955, gift of P.T. Brooke Sewell
Brass engraved and inlaid with silver
H 20.3 cm
BM 1955,0214.1

This candlestick holder is made of cast brass inlaid with silver and gold. On the body of the candlestick the decoration includes a medallion showing a horseman slaying a lion with a sword. On the socket there are representations of musicians.

142

Base of a waterpipe or *galiyan*

17th century AD
Kerman, Iran; presented by A.W. Franks in 1890
Stone-paste ceramic with underglaze painted decoration
H 29.3 cm. Diam. 18.7 cm
BM 1890.0517.13

This is the base of a *huqqa*, or waterpipe, known as a *galiyan* in Persia. Tobacco smoke is passed through water in this container before being inhaled. The polychrome painted decoration shows scenes from the story of Khusrow and Shirin immortalized by the twelfth-century Persian poet Nizami. The story is based on the life of the Sasanian king Khusrow II. In one scene Khusrow is shown out hunting on horseback, with a quiver behind him and a falcon perched on his gloved hand. In another scene, a semi-naked Shirin is bathing in a stream, but Khusrow does not realize she is the beautiful Armenian princess his vizier has described to him.

Glazed tile showing a polo match

c. AD 1850, Qajar
Tehran, Iran; Godman bequest, 1983
Stone-paste ceramic with underglaze painted decoration
H 30.6 cm, W 30.6 cm
BM G.314

The scene on this tile is from the Persian epic the *Shahnameh* and shows a polo match between Siyavash and Afrasiyab. Siyavash had fled to the court of Afrasiyab (King of Turan) after a dispute with his father, the king of Iran. The story is described in a Persian inscription around the edge of the tile. The cartouches at the top contain the name of the potter, Muhammad Ibrahim.

144

A Mughal nobleman on horseback

Rembrandt van Rijn (1606–1669)
c. 1656–61; Mordaunt Cracherode bequest, 1799
Ink on paper
H 20.5 cm, W 17.7 cm
BM Gg.2.262

Rembrandt was known to have produced a series of
twenty-one drawings inspired by Mughal miniatures,
many of which originally came from the court of Shah
Jahan (reigned 1627–1658). Several of his drawings are
similar to the Mughal vignettes found on the walls of the
'Million Room' at Schönbrunn Castle, Vienna.

   This drawing shows a Mughal nobleman, probably
Shah Jahan, on horseback, holding the reins in his
left hand and a lance in his right. It is unclear where
Rembrandt copied this drawing from, but as with most
of his Mughal images, he has not drawn a background
and has probably left out some details, such as the
tassel that would have hung from the horse's neck strap
(as seen in cats 145, 146, 151).

145

Copy of miniature painting in the Bodleian Library

1630
H 26.3 cm, W 17.2 cm
Bodleian Library, MS. Douce Or. a.1: fol. 25.a

This miniature shows Shah Jahan riding his horse
and holding a lance, much like the figure shown in
Rembrandt's drawing. In this example one can see the
details that have been left out of Rembrandt's work, such
as the horse's neck-strap tassel. While this work has not
been identified as that which influenced Rembrandt, it
demonstrates that his drawing would have been inspired
by an existing Mughal piece.

   This image is from an album of forty-one Indian
paintings, chiefly from the Shah Jahan period (1627–1658).

146

Two men in Persian costume shoeing a horse

c. 1600, Mughal
India
Ink, opaque watercolour, silver and gold on paper
H 12.4 cm, W 14.2 cm
BM 1942,0124,0.1

This painting depicts two men shoeing a horse, while a third man holds its head. The horse is shoed by a bearded man wearing Persian costume. The horse itself wears a saddle and harness fittings, including a large red-tasselled neck strap. This finely drawn composition has been attributed to Kesu Das, a leading painter at the courts of the Mughal emperors Akbar and Jahangir. The majority of his known works are based on European prints, but he also produced manuscript illustrations and portraits. This drawing exemplifies the Mughal interest in naturalism as it includes all the tools needed for shoeing a horse.

147

Battle between Khusrow Parviz and Bahram VI

Late 15th century, Turkman
Iran
Ink, opaque watercolour and gold on paper
H 14.8 cm, W 20 cm
BM 1925,0902,0.1

This scene from the *Shahnameh* shows a battle between the
Sasanian kings Khusrow II (590–AD 628) and Bahram VI (590–AD 1).
Khusrow Parviz gained the throne after his weak father, Hormuzd,
was blinded by his own brothers. The most powerful soldier in
the land and a descendant of an earlier dynasty, Bahram Chubin
(Bahram VI) was a claimant to the throne. After routing Khusrow
Parviz in battle, Bahram pursued him westwards, but eventually
Khusrow was victorious and Bahram fled to China. The soldiers
in this battle are mounted, fighting with lances and swords. At the
upper right of this illustration a trumpeter blows a long horn with
a bend in its shaft, which is a variation on the *karna* with a straight
shaft. These trumpets and various types of kettle drums were
integral to military bands which accompanied armies in battle and
played in processions and other ceremonies.

148

Princely figure on horseback with a falcon

Early 18th century
India, possibly Delhi
Ink, opaque watercolour and gold on paper
H 55.8 cm, W 40.4 cm
BM 1920,0917,0.88.1

A man is shown on horseback, with a falcon perched on his gloved right hand as he holds the reins in his bare left hand. The horse has a finely shaped head, with an arched neck. This may actually be a posthumous representation of the emperor Shah Jahan (reigned 1628–1658) or a copy of an earlier portrait of the great Mughal ruler.

157

Helmet (*çikaç*)

Turkish, 16th century, modified for use in Sudan, late 19th century
Bequest of Dr R. Williams, 1974
H (of skull) 28.7 cm, H (overall) 52 cm, Diam. (of skull)
c. 23.5 cm
Steel and textile
Royal Armouries, XXVIA.119

The faceted conical skull of this helmet is elegantly engraved with scrolling foliage. Its original peak has been lost and replaced with a later one, at the same time as the threaded bracket for the lost nasal defence was replaced. The quilted textile lining is typical of those fitted to Sudanese helmets, and the mail aventail (hood), which was most likely fitted at the same time as the lining, is European, cut from a fifteenth-century mail shirt.

158

Quilted suit of armour

19th century
Sudan; acquired 1899, gift of M. Maxse
Cotton, fibre
L 138 cm, W 130 cm
BM 1899,1231.1

Suit of quilted textile armour worn by a horseman (probably a Dervish warrior), with bands of red and dark blue colour on a natural ground and black edging.

159

Armour for horse and rider

Late 15th century, Turkish
Original pieces all from Hagia Irene, Istanbul (Helmet
purchased, 1841; coat on loan to the Royal Armouries
from the Royal Collection; horse armour purchased
1992, formerly in the collection of Frank Gair
Macomber)
Steel
Royal Armouries, XXVIA.116, XXVIA.222, XXVIH.33–5

Mail and plate armour for man and horse
became the standard type of equipment for the
heavy cavalry under the Timurids (1370–1506),
the Mongol successor empire which ruled from
Samarkand, and under the Ottoman Turks.
Such heavy cavalry, armed with bow, sword and
sometimes lance, were the main component of
all the medieval Islamic armies.

Horse armours of mail and plate appear
relatively common among Islamic cavalry
of the fifteenth century, judging by artistic
representations, but this example is one of only
seventeen to survive today. It and the mail and
plate armour for the man (*zirh gomlek*) lack all
the quilted textile linings with which they were
originally fitted. The helmet is probably south
Russian, modified into a Turkish *çikaç* with
additional neckguard and cheekpieces. The
armour is supplemented by modern replicas
of sword (*kılıç*) and scabbard, bow, bow-case
and quiver, and shield (*kalkan*) to give a vivid
impression of heavy cavalry equipment.

190

Horse and Horseman

Ahmed Moustafa
1996–8
Mixed oil and acrylic on canvas
H 200 cm, W 162 cm
King Abdulaziz Public Library

Although it bears a superficial resemblance to equestrian portraits in the European tradition, this remarkable painting by Ahmed Moustafa is a unique work of art in a genre invented by the artist. The whole composition consists of Arabic letters derived from literary works which have inspired the artist, including poems in praise of the horse by Imru' al-Qays and Al Muzarrid ibn Dirar and poems in praise of King Abdul Aziz ibn Saud by Abbas Mahmud al-Aqqad and Ibn al-Uthaymin. Although this painting is not intended as a formal portrait, it was inspired by the achievements of King Abdul Aziz ibn Saud who is often regarded as the last person to unite a kingdom on horseback. This culminated in the creation of the State of Saudi Arabia in 1932. In the words of Jeremy Henzell-Thomas who has written a booklet about this painting based on an interview with Ahmed Moustafa, 'This is the portrait not of a historical monarch exulting in his own triumph, but an idealized representation of an archetypal horse and horseman expressing the universal attributes associated with the Arab horse, that aristocrat of horses, and its noble rider, who epitomises manliness (*muru'ah*) and chivalry (*futuwwah*).' The same composition has also been reproduced on a tapestry woven in France.

191

Photograph of Lady Anne Blunt

H 11.5 cm, W 17.5 cm
Fitzwilliam Museum, PH 27-2004

In this photograph Lady Anne Blunt is shown in Arabian dress
standing at the head of her dark-coloured Arabian mare
Kasida at her home, Crabbet Park.

205
Miseries of London

Thomas Rowlandson
1807
Hand-coloured etching with stipple
H 27.5 cm, W 37.1 cm
Collection of Nicholas Knowles

A street-scene based on Beresford's *Miseries of Human Life* (1806), illustrating lines which follow the title of the design: 'In going out to dinner (already too late) your carriage delayed by a jam of coaches – which choak up the whole street and allow you at least an hour or more than you require to sharpen your wits for table talk.'

Coaches are shown in a traffic jam on a busy London street, with a carriage driving to the right, tipping to one side, to the consternation of the passengers, the driver raising his whip against the driver of a carriage travelling in the opposite direction, whose passenger is a buxom woman, leaning out of the window in distress. The spire of St Giles can be seen in the distance on the left. At this time horses were extensively used to pull carriages and cabs in the streets of London.

MISERIES OF LONDON.
In going out to dinner (already too late) your carriage delayed by a jam of coaches — which choak up the whole street. and allow you at least an hour or more than you require. to sharpen your wits for table talk.
" Breast against breast with ruinous assault
" And deafning shock. they come —

Pub.d Feb.y 1st 1807 by R Ackerman N.o 101 Strand

THE CAMBRIDGE TELEGRAPH,
STARTING FROM THE WHITE HORSE, FETTER LANE.

206

The Cambridge Telegraph

George Hunt
1825–36
Hand-coloured aquatint with etching
H 43.6 cm, W 55 cm
BM 1880,1113.4311

A view of the London to Cambridge mail coach about to depart outside the White Horse Tavern at night, with passengers on top and inside the carriage.

Horses were yoked in teams of four to pull mail coaches over long distances. At this time, the journey from London to Cambridge took about five hours. The use of horses for travel and mail delivery was essential until the late 1830s, when the rail network was widely developed, providing faster journey times. The last regular national mail coach delivery was made in 1846, from London to Norwich, via Newmarket.

207

A Representation of the Persians in the Costume of their Country, Attending at Carlton Palace, with portraits of the horses presented to His Majesty by His Excellency the Ambassador from the Emperor of Persia

Henry Bernard Chalon (1770–1849)
1819
Oil on canvas
H 101 cm, W 144 cm
Tate, T02357; presented by Paul Mellon through the British
Sporting Art Trust, 1979

Chalon exhibited a picture with this title at the British
Institution in 1820. The exhibited picture is likely to have
been the more highly finished version signed and dated
1819, reputedly commissioned by George IV (at that
time Prince Regent) but not paid for, and subsequently
purchased by Major Bower, by whose descendants it was
sold at Sotheby's on 17 November 1976. This painting
may be either a preliminary version or a replica painted
for an unknown admirer of the exhibited picture.

The painting shows eight Arabian horses to be
presented to George III by the ambassador of Fath-'Ali
Shah of Persia in 1819. The purpose of the mission was
to discuss with Lord Castlereagh certain aspects of the
Anglo-Persian treaty concluded by Sir Gore Ouseley in
Tehran in 1812. During his visit, the Persian Ambassador
was taken to Epsom races.

212

Eclipse

John N. Sartorius (1759–1828)
1790
Oil on canvas
H 71 cm, W 92 cm
Jockey Club Estates

This portrait was painted a year after the death of Eclipse, probably based
on a drawing by Francis Sartorius, the artist's father. Eclipse (1764–1789)
was an undefeated Thoroughbred racehorse who was also distinguished
as a sire. He is sometimes referred to as the greatest horse ever to appear
on British turf.

213

Eclipse

Thomas Burke (1749–1815), after George Stubbs (1724–1806)

1772

Mezzotint

H 46 cm, W 56.5 cm

BM 1854,1020.26

This print is after a painting by George Stubbs (*c.* 1770) and shows Eclipse being held by a groom, as his jockey, John Oakley, approaches. They are standing outside one of the four 'rubbing-down houses' that stood at Newmarket Heath during the eighteenth century. These houses were used for rubbing down sweaty horses with pieces of straw or cloths after exercising or racing, as seen in another of Stubbs's paintings, *Hambeltonian, Rubbing Down* (1800).

Tom Merry del et lith

214

The Eclipse Stakes: The Finish

Tom Merry (pseudonym for William Mecham, 1853–1902)
1886
Lithograph
H 47.4 cm, W 30 cm
BM 1945,0109.38

The bottom of this print shows the finish of the first ever Eclipse Stakes, named after the racehorse Eclipse, held at Sandown Park on Friday 23 July 1886. This race was attended by HRH the Prince of Wales, later Edward VII. At the top of the print we can see a rather stern-looking William Ewart Gladstone depicted as the moon and Lord Salisbury (Robert Gascoyne-Cecil) depicted as the sun. It is written in the accompanying text that: 'it has since transpired that just as the race was being run HRH had seen a vision in the sky – of a luminous body emerging from behind the eclipsing shade of a black and opaque mass. These bodies had shaped themselves, as he thought, into the faces of leading statesmen.' Thus, Salisbury is here seen as the sun emerging from the darkness of Gladstone, a prediction that pre-empts his re-election as Prime Minister a month later in August that year.

219

The Derby Day

William Powell Frith (1819–1909)
1856–8
H 101.6 cm, W 223.5 cm
Oil on canvas
Tate, N00615; bequeathed by Jacob Bell, 1859

Even within the seemingly limitless quantity of nineteenth-century sporting art, William Powell Frith's *The Derby Day* is unrivalled both for its visual impact and for illustrating the immense popularity and appeal of horseracing across all sections of Victorian society.

Frith's achievement in this multi-layered work, cast within the popular genre of a panorama of contemporary life, is in highlighting current social and moral concerns and themes through a partly documentary and partly satirical approach, while simultaneously celebrating the phenomena of racing as a great event unifying all people and classes. Through easily recognizable stereotypes of simple countryfolk led astray, ordinary racegoers and outsiders on the fringes of acceptable society (travellers, acrobats, wealthy

transgressors and courtesans) Frith both reassured and challenged his audience.

Remarkably, the painting's history mirrors these same themes, illuminating what may now seem the unexpectedly interlocking social networks within Victorian society. The painting's origin and success linked artists, the world of business and politics, equestrian sport and royal circles, and the growing popular interest in contemporary art (and the new fortunes to be made from it). *The Derby Day* was commissioned by Frith's close friend Jacob Bell (1810–1859) for £1,500 on the basis of an unfinished sketch. Bell, a Quaker by upbringing, was the owner of an established pharmaceutical business, a founder of the Pharmaceutical Society of Great

Britain and a sometime MP (whose normal for the time but unfortunately inept bribery to secure his St Albans seat precipitated eventual bribery reform). Yet Bell was also an enthusiast of art and the turf who had attended the same art school as Frith, who procured Frith's female models, and acted as the unofficial business agent of his great friend Edwin Henry Landseer (1802–1873), the immensely popular animal artist and royal favourite. The dealer Ernest Gambart bought the copyright and exhibition rights anticipating the immense popularity of the subject and the sale of engravings in large numbers.Such was the enthusiasm for the painting when it was shown at the Royal Academy in May 1858 that a rail was erected to keep the crowds away from it.

Grand Stand Ascot: Gold Cup Day 1839

Charles Hunt (1803–1877), after John Frederick Herring (1795–1865)
1839; acquired 1949, gift of Edward Croft-Murray
Hand-coloured engraving and aquatint
H 62 cm, W 79.5 cm
BM 1949,0217.31

The black horse in the foreground appears to be being prepared for the race, with his jockey standing behind it carrying the saddle and a groom removing the horse's blanket, while another groom holds it steady. The movement of the other horses in this scene indicates the tension and energy before the race begins. In the background is the Grand Stand and enclosure, packed with racegoers. To the right of the Grand Stand is the Royal Box, which is flying the Royal Standard, indicating Queen Victoria's presence at the race.

The first Grand Stand at Ascot opened in 1839, after a year of construction, and it was able to hold up to 1200 people on the ground floor and 1800 on the roof. The winner of the Gold Cup that year was Caravan, a descendant of Eclipse and the Darley Arabian.

This print is after John Frederick Herring who counted Queen Victoria as his patron.

Grand Stand, Ascot.
(GOLD CUP DAY 1839)

221

Epsom: The Race Over

Charles Hunt (1803–1877), after James Pollard (1792–1867)
1836; acquired 1933, gift of C.F.G.R. Schwerdt
Hand-coloured etching and aquatint
H 33.6 cm, W 46.2 cm
BM 1933,1014.103

The scene here shows the end of the race, with jockeys dismounting their
horses and removing their saddles in the foreground. In the background is a
large crowd, being kept back by men in dark coats and white trousers. Either
side of the centre are stands and enclosures, still crowded with people.

    The Epsom Derby in 1836 was won by Bay Middleton, a descendant of
Herod and the Byerley Turk.

Sir Harry Tempest Vane's Horse HAMBLETONIAN, Preparing to Start against Mr Cookson's DIAMOND, over the Beacon Course at NEWMARKET, for a Match of THREE THOUSAND GUINEAS, a Side, half forfeit. Hambletonian carried 8:3, and was rode by Mr He. Diamond was rode by Mr Dennis Fitzpatrick and 2nd 8. This Race was run at the Craven Meeting on Monday March 25 1799.

222

Hambletonian and Diamond at Newmarket

John Whessell (c. 1760–1806), after J.N. Sartorius (1759–1828)
1800; acquired 1917, gift of N.I. Cooper in memory of A.T. Herbert
Hand-coloured stipple and etching
H 38.9 cm, W 53.8 cm
BM 1917,1208.2434

This print shows the moments before the famous Craven Meeting between Hambletonian, owned by Sir Henry Tempest Vane, and Diamond, owned by Mr Cookson. The two horses are seen making their way to the starting post on the left, with their jockeys mounted, and to the right is the rubbing down-house. Hambletonian, on the left, is ridden by Mr Buckle, who wears a dark hat, white breeches and a blue jacket with yellow sleeves, while Diamond's jockey, Mr Fitzpatrick, wears a yellow hat, white breeches and a blue jacket.

At this early stage in horseracing, matches were often arranged between pairs of horses rather than a group of them. The text below the scene states that this race took place on 25 March 1799 at the Beacon Course and was for the sum of three thousand guineas. Hambletonian, whose grandsire was Eclipse, narrowly beat Diamond, whose grandsire was Herod, to the finish.

223

Commemorative token

1799; acquired 1907, gift of Montague Guest
Silver
Diam. 3.6 cm
BM MG.1191

The obverse shows two racehorses with the inscription 'Hambletonian Diamond'; and the reverse has the inscription 'No. 3 King's Place, Pall Mall'. This counter commemorates the famous race between Hambletonian and Diamond in 1799 (see cat. 222).

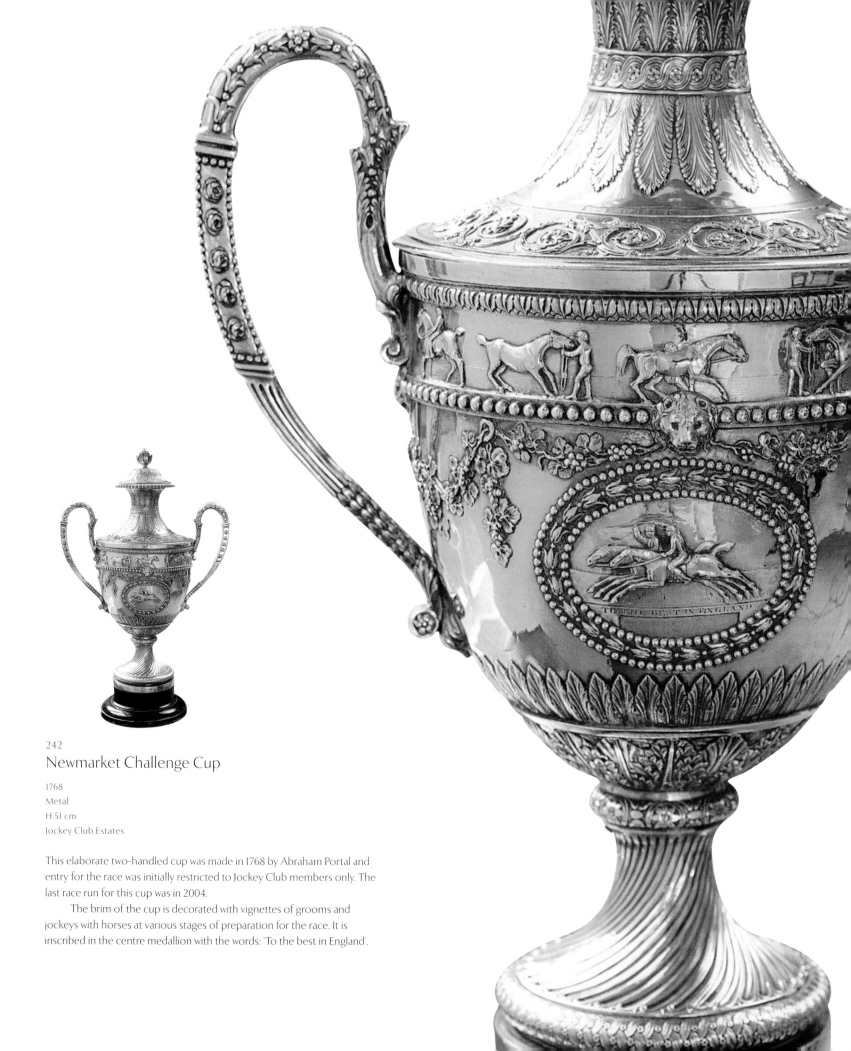

242

Newmarket Challenge Cup

1768
Metal
H 51 cm
Jockey Club Estates

This elaborate two-handled cup was made in 1768 by Abraham Portal and entry for the race was initially restricted to Jockey Club members only. The last race run for this cup was in 2004.

The brim of the cup is decorated with vignettes of grooms and jockeys with horses at various stages of preparation for the race. It is inscribed in the centre medallion with the words: 'To the best in England'.

Fig. 48
Queen Elizabeth II's horse Free
Agent wins the Chesham Stakes
at Royal Ascot on 21 June 2008,
ridden by Richard Hughes.

Further reading

Penguin Classics translation of the Koran by N.J. Dawood (1956)

David Alexander (ed.), *Furusiyya, vol. 1, The Horse in the Art of the Near East*, vol. 2, *Catalogue* (Riyadh 1996).

HRH Princess Alia al Hussein and Peter Upton, *Royal Heritage: the Story of Jordan's Arab Horses* (Newport, Isle of Wight, 2011)

Hossein Amirsadegh (with an introduction by HH Sheikh Zayed bin-Sultan al-Nahyan), *The Arabian Horse: History, Mystery and Magic* (London 1998)

Lady Anne Blunt, *Bedouin Tribes of the Euphrates* (London 1879)

Lady Anne Blunt, *A Pilgrimage to Nejd* (London 1881)

Johann L Burckhardt, *Travels in Arabia* (London 1829)

J. Clutton-Brock and S. Davies, 'More donkeys from Tell Brak', *Iraq* LV (1993), pp. 209–21

J.E. Curtis and J.E. Reade (eds), *Art and Empire: Treasures from Assyria in the British Museum* (London 1995)

J.E. Curtis and N. Tallis, *Forgotten Empire: the World of Ancient Persia* (London 2005)

Geoff Emberling and Helen McDonald, 'Excavations at Tell Brak 2001–2002: preliminary report', *Iraq* LXV (2003), pp. 1–75

Judith Forbis and Gülsün Sherif, *The Abbas Pasha Manuscript and Horses and Horsemen of Arabia and Egypt during the Time of Abbas Pasha 1800–1860* (Mena, Arkansas, 1993)

Robert G Hoyland, *Arabia and the Arabs* (London 2001)

M.A. Littauer and J.H. Crouwel, *Wheeled Vehicles and Ridden Animals in the Ancient Near East* (Leiden/Köln 1979)

Elizabeth Longford, *Pilgrimage of Passion: The Life of Wilfrid Scawen Blunt* (London 1979)

Nasr Marei and Cynthia Culbertson, *The Arabian Horse of Egypt* (Cairo 2010)

David Oldrey, *The Jockey Club Rooms: a Catalogue and History of the Collection* (London 2006)

S.L. Olsen and C. Culbertson, *A Gift from the Desert: The Art, History and Culture of the Arabian Horse* (Lexington, Kentucky 2010)

William G Palgrave, *Personal Narrative of a Year's Journey through Central and Eastern Arabia (1862–1863)* (London 1865)

Carl R. Raswan, *Drinkers of the Wind: the Amazing Story of the Steeds of the Arabian Desert* (London 1938)

Fred Rice, Chestnuts, *Greys and Rodeo Days: My Life at Crabbet Park* (Worth, Sussex 1993).

G. Rex Smith, *Medieval Muslim Horsemanship: a Fourteenth-Century Arabic Cavalry Manual* (London 1979)

Keith Thomas, *Man and the Natural World: Changing Attitudes in England 1500–1800* (London 1984)

Peter Upton, *Out of the Desert: the Influence of the Arab Horse on the Light Horse and Native Pony Breeds of Britain* (Newport, Isle of Wight, 2010)

Peter Upton, *The Arab Horse* (Newport, Isle of Wight, 2012)

Malcolm Warner and Robin Blake, *Stubbs and the Horse* (New Haven and London 2004)

Judith, Baroness Wentworth (1945) *The Authentic Arabian Horse and his Descendants* (London 1945)

H.V.F. Winstone, *Lady Anne Blunt: A Biography* (London 2003)

Illustration acknowledgements

The publishers would like to thank the copyright holders for granting permission to reproduce the images illustrated. Every attempt has been made to trace accurate ownership of copyrighted images in this book. Errors and omissions will be corrected in subsequent editions provided notification is sent to the publisher.

All photographs of British Museum objects are © The Trustees of the British Museum, courtesy of the Department of Photography and Imaging. Map artwork © The Trustees of the British Museum (artwork by Matt Bigg at Surface 3)

Half-title page: Supplied by Royal Collection Trust / © HM Queen Elizabeth II 2012
Fig. 8 © Superstock
Fig. 10 John Curtis
Fig. 14 Private Collection / Archives Charmet / The Bridgeman Art Library
Fig. 16 The British Library Board (Add 18866)
Fig. 17 The British Library Board (Add 18866)
Fig. 20 Richard T. Bryant
Fig. 22 Richard T. Bryant
Fig. 23 Richard T. Bryant
Fig. 24 © Latif Al Obaida
Fig. 25 © Latif Al Obaida
Fig. 26 The British Library Board (Add 53893)
Fig. 27 The British Library Board (Add 54055)
Fig. 28 The British Library Board (Add 54085B)
Fig. 29 From C.R. Raswan, *Drinkers of the Wind* (London 1938), facing p. 224
Fig. 31 The British Library Board (Add 54085B)
Fig. 32 The British Library Board (Add 54085B)
Fig. 33 Peter Upton
Fig. 34 The British Library Board (Add 54141)
Fig. 35 The British Library Board (Add 54085B)
Fig. 36 Alan Crowhurst / Getty Images
Fig. 37 Supplied by Royal Collection Trust / © HM Queen Elizabeth II 2012

Fig. 38 Tate, London 2012
Fig. 39 Christie's Images Ltd, 2012
Fig. 41 The Bodleian Library, University of Oxford (Harding B 25 [1784]; Harding B 6 [54])
Fig. 42 Supplied by Royal Collection Trust / © HM Queen Elizabeth II 2012
Fig. 43 Press Association
Fig. 44 Carl Court / Getty Images
Fig. 45 Reproduced by permission of the Vorderasiatisches Museum, Berlin.
Cat. 3 Drawing after S. Smith, An Early Painted Vase from Khafaji, *British Museum Quarterly*, VIII, 1933–4, p. 39, fig. 1
Cat. 37 © The Trustees of the British Museum (artwork by Kate Morton)
Fig. 47 Drawing after R. Campbell Thompson and R. W. Hutchinson, 'The Site of the Palace of Ashurnasirpal at Nineveh, excavated in 1929–30 on behalf of the British Museum', in *Annals of Archaeology and Anthropology*, vol. XVIII, 1931, pl. XVIII.
Cat. 47 Drawing © The Trustees of the British Museum (drawing by Ann Searight)
Cat. 105 Drawing © The Trustees of the British Museum (drawing by Ann Searight)
Cat. 106 Drawing after O.M. Dalton, The Treasure of the Oxus (London, 1964), p.15, Fig. 49
Cats 129–32 King Abdulaziz Public Library
Cat. 133 King King Abdulaziz Public Library
Cat. 134 The British Library Board (Add 18866)
Cat. 145 The Bodleian Library, University of Oxford (MS Douce Or. a. 1: fol. 25.a)
Cat. 155 Image courtesy of Jila Peacock
Cat. 157 Bridgeman Art Library / Royal Armouries, Leeds
Cat. 159 Royal Armouries, Leeds
Cat. 164 Richard T. Bryant
Cats 165–80 National Museum of Saudi Arabia
Cat. 181 King Saud University Museum
Cat. 182 National Museum of Saudi Arabia

Cat. 183 King Saud University Museum
Cat. 189 King Abdulaziz Public Library
Cat. 190 King Abdulaziz Public Library
Cat. 191 © The Fitzwilliam Museum, Cambridge (PH 27-2004)
Cat. 192 The British Library Board (Add 54131)
Cat. 193 The British Library Board (Add 54109)
Cat. 194 The British Library Board (Add 54109)
Cat. 195 The British Library Board (Add 53890)
Cat. 196 The British Library Board (Add 53893)
Cat. 197 The British Library Board (Add 54076)
Cat. 198 © The Fitzwilliam Museum, Cambridge (PH 16-2004)
Cat. 199 © The Fitzwilliam Museum, Cambridge (PH 124-2004 (1-2))
Cat. 200 © The Fitzwilliam Museum, Cambridge (MS.30–1975)
Cat. 204 Supplied by Royal Collection Trust / © HM Queen Elizabeth II 2012
Cat. 205 Reproduced by permission of Nicholas Knowles
Cat. 207 Tate, London 2012
Cat. 208 Supplied by Royal Collection Trust / © HM Queen Elizabeth II 2012
Cat. 211 © Private Collection at the National Horseracing Museum
Cat. 212 Jockey Club Estates
Cat. 218 © The Fitzwilliam Museum, Cambridge (PD 7-1982)
Cat. 219 Tate, London 2012
Cat. 225 Supplied by Royal Collection Trust / © HM Queen Elizabeth II 2012
Cat. 241 Courtesy of Prince Khalid Abdullah
Cat. 242 Jockey Club Estates
Fig. 48 (p. 258) Julian Herbert / Getty Images
Cats 243–4 Supplied by Royal Collection Trust / All rights reserved
Cat. 246 The Layan Foundation
Cat. 249 IOC
Cat. 252 photo McCabe / Getty Images
Cat. 256 Courtesy of HRH Prince Khalid bin Abdullah